— Praise for —

SECRETS OF A WORKING DOG

"Bella shares a unique perspective on life, work and the pursuit of success as only a dog could tell it. Secrets of a Working Dog *contains practical, real-world wisdom to which every dog owner can relate and that every entrepreneur and business person should read."*

Cathy King, DVM PhD, CEO of World Vets

"A dog-author who deeply understands the power of 'pawsitive' thinking, Bella (with a little help from her humans) has written a charming, fun, and thoughtful book that can help us all live better."

Rick Foster, co-author of *How We Choose to Be Happy* and *Happiness & Health*

"Two paws up! Bella the Boxer has crafted a fun and creative look at what it takes to be successful in today's business climate. Like any dog who wants off the leash, Bella holds nothing back—the stories, examples, and unique perspective make this book an easy but powerful read."

Richard Fenton and Andrea Waltz, authors of *Go for No!*

"Since dogs have been interacting with humans for thousands of years, it was just a matter of time before an entrepreneurial one decided to offer observations on how we humans work and live. I'm glad it was Bella since her effective storytelling and savvy ideas take people looking to better themselves on an interesting walk of self-discovery."

Paul Witkay, founder and CEO of the Alliance of Chief Executives

"Bella has great ideas for building relationships and motivating people. I especially like her views on happiness—she's sort of the Doggie Dalai Lama."

Dyana King, CEO of Thinknicity Inc.

"Bella delivers the goods. Her wise and witty observations and personal glimpse into the lives of dogs gives us a window to peek through and a door to enter. Cheers, woofs, and wags to the irrepressible Bella and to the people with whom she shares her life. Through them, an utterly charming and thought-provoking book has been born."

Corinne Dowling, founder of Give a Dog a Bone

"You don't need a dog to appreciate the business message in this book. The lessons in each chapter are compelling and will help anyone interested in improving their ability to relate to other people. What a mixture of humor and wisdom: I couldn't put the book down!"

Pat Murphy, president of Reid Industries

"I'm a cat lover but Bella is one smart dogpreneur. I wish I'd had Bella on the end of my leash when I started my business. This is a fresh, fun and enlightening business book. The stories illustrate sound business advice and emphasize how each person's idea of success is different."

Susan Urquhart-Brown, business coach and author of *The Accidental Entrepreneur: 50 Things I Wish Someone Had Told Me About Starting a Business*

"Bella has a direct and unabashed perspective on everything from work to play. Those of us lucky enough to share our time with dogs will appreciate Bella's simple and genuine suggestions for living an authentic life, from the time we wake up to the time we cuddle up. She'll change your perspective, your attitude, and your confidence. Bravo, Bella!"

Bob Stonhaus, inventor of the STORViNO wine storage system

SECRETS OF A WORKING DOG

*Unleash Your Potential
and Create Success*

Patrick Galvin

Bella

Ellen Galvin

SECRETS OF A WORKING DOG

*Unleash Your Potential
and Create Success*

by Bella the Boxer

With Ellen Galvin and Patrick Galvin

JRP
JOSEPH RUDOLPH PUBLISHERS

Published by Joseph Rudolph Publishers.

JRP
JOSEPH RUDOLPH PUBLISHERS

4133 NE 32nd Place
Portland, Oregon 97211
info@josephrudolphpublishers.com

For discounts on bulk orders or to book the author(s)
for a speaking engagement, contact the publisher.
Although the authors have made every effort to provide accu-
rate Internet addresses at the time of publication, they do not
assume any responsibility for errors or changes that occur
after publication. Further, they do not have any control over
and do not assume any responsibility for third-party websites
or their content.

Library of Congress Control Number 2010911914
ISBN: 978-0-9828680-3-4
E-Book ISBN: 978-0-9828680-4-1

. . . .

I dedicate this book to my two-legged,
2-year-old sister, Anya, who makes sure
that I'm never without food and who
thinks that all dogs are named Bella.

Contents

Author's Note

I am a dog named Bella. This is a book written by a dog. As such, you won't find me referring to my fellow canines as "it," but rather "he" or "she," pronouns that I interchange at will except when referring to a specific canine.

Also, if you are a beagle who takes offense because "beagle" is lowercase and "Maltese" is uppercase, let me explain that the generally accepted rule of capitalization for dog breeds is that if the breed is named after a place or a person, it is capitalized. Obviously, it's not my rule or else "boxer" would be capitalized. But I've gotten over it, and I hope that you will, too.

When it comes to describing my own family unit, I alternate between describing them as "my humans," "my two-legged humans" and "Mom and Dad." For anyone who thinks this is sappy and infantile, I apologize—but you should consider yourself lucky that I don't call them "Mommy and Daddy."

Finally, there are all sorts of semantics surrounding the human-animal relationship. Some communities have enacted ordinances that change "owners" into "guardians." Others encourage people to refer to their animals as "companions" instead of "pets." I'm going to stay out of that debate. Whichever word you choose, humans are responsible for the care and well-being of the animals they have domesticated. Gandhi had it right when he said that "The greatness of a nation and its moral progress can be judged by the way its animals are treated."

Foreword

by Zelda the Bulldog

One of the greatest things about being a dog is having a free pass to give humans the kind of straightforward, no-bull (bulldog, that is) advice that they don't often hear from each other. There's something about our soulful eyes and fuzzy muzzles that gets humans to sit up and pay attention.

Pedigrees don't matter, either. All canines are guide dogs in one way or another and we all have something valuable to teach the people around us—provided they are willing to listen, of course. Take me, for example. I have short, stubby legs, a serious underbite, and wrinkles that would defy the best plastic surgeon in Beverly Hills. And yet I've been doling out advice to humans for well over a decade on topics that range from romance to parenting and weight watching to philosophy. I've taught millions of people about the power of humor and convinced them that we don't have to be perfect to create meaningful and happy lives.

In my advice column, I've answered a lot of questions from overworked and underappreciated humans. So I know that people are struggling to balance the challenges of modern life in a world that is always plugged-in and turned "on." That's why it's so nice to hear another voice of reason. In this book, my buddy Bella tells it like it is. She teaches people to focus on what's important, and to create their own success instead of sitting on their haunches and hoping that something magic will happen—like finding a dog bowl that never runs out of calorie-free kibble (okay, I'm projecting one of my biggest fantasies here).

Of course, Bella's success as a guru makes perfect sense when you consider that the boxer is a direct descendant of the English bulldog. I guess this explains why we are both stubborn individualists, as well as loyal and lovable companions. More important, Bella inherited the wit and wisdom for which my breed is known, not to mention the entrepreneurial savvy and stunning good looks. She's sharp and funny, and gets people to laugh at themselves while learning valuable life lessons.

Look, I know how hard it is for some people—especially cat people—to overcome their skepticism and take advice from a dog. I've walked a similar path as a 'dogpreneur,' but I like to think that I helped pave the way for smart and sassy canines like Bella to help people achieve their full human potential. So whether or not you share your life with a dog, *Secrets of a Working Dog* will help you unleash your own potential and discover what it means to become a success.

Woofs, wags, and a little wisdom,

Zelda
CEO of Zelda Wisdom, Inc.
www.zeldawisdom.com

"All knowledge, the totality of
all questions and all answers,
is contained in the dog."

– Franz Kafka

Success and
a New Breed
of Working Dog

Success is not the key to happiness.
Happiness is the key to success. If you love what
you are doing, you will be successful.

– Herman Cain

"Where are the dogs going?" you people who pay so
little attention ask. They are going about their business.
And they are very punctilious, without wallets, notes,
and without briefcases.

– Charles Baudelaire

My name is Bella and I am a boxer. I'm also a dogpreneur, and, like opinionated, self-confident dogpreneurs everywhere, I consider myself a success.

But what is success, really? There is no one-size-fits-all method for raising and training a dog, and there is no standard for achieving personal or professional success. Humans often think success comes from knowledge, experience, respect, relationships, confidence, money, fame or even a combination of these wonderful things. But dogs know that true success comes from one thing: living an authentic and well-balanced life. How do you get it? It starts by following your instincts.

Success also requires time, energy and commitment—things that most people don't feel they have room for in our fast-paced, hyper-connected world. People use the expression "working like a dog" to describe toiling away at a pointless task or job, hoping for something better to come along. Of course, they're forgetting that a dog at work has self-confidence, focus and purpose. A dog at work zeroes in on what's important in life and filters out what's not. A dog at work is a success.

PAVLOV'S PEOPLE

Dogs are happiest when their two-legged friends are happy. But how does someone get happy? Too many people are overworked and overstressed, chasing someone else's idea of success instead of stopping to dig deeper and pursue their own personal plans for happiness. They begin to believe that success is beyond their reach, creating additional frustration and stress.

Obviously, it's impossible to have a completely stress-free life. Stress can even be good in short bursts. It boosts the immune system and helps the body recover and repair itself more quickly. When an evil squirrel invades the back-yard, for example, it's stress that gets my heart beating faster and my legs pumping quicker. Stress tells my body what to do, i.e., get that squirrel! See, stress can be fun!

On the other hand, long-term emotional stress takes a toll on your body and your mind. Too many people associate stress with status, as in "The busier I am the more important I am." And although I hate to burst your bubble, busy does *not* equal productive. You can talk, type, text or tweet to the point of exhaustion and still not get anything meaningful done. Pavlov's salivating dogs don't hold a candle to the packs of people who drool at every "beep," "ding" or "buzz" that comes from their laptops, cell phones and BlackBerries.

Right now you're probably asking yourself, "How would a dog know this stuff?" Humans naively think that their canine companions spend the entire day sleeping. However, dogs have heightened senses, so we don't need to keep our eyes open to know what you're doing. We hear you tapping the "Send/Receive" button in your e-mail inbox over and over (and over again). Plus one peek and we know from your body language when you've logged on to Facebook, clicked over to *ESPN.com* or, in my human's case, wasted an hour chuckling over *I Can Has Cheezburger* (a website that should be banned from all workplaces because it's about cats, of all things).

Notice, if you please, that all those electronic "time-savers" and "fun" diversions don't seem to be making people particularly happy or productive. Being connected 24/7 has just created too many people who are tense, irritable, distracted and depressed. Sure, many of you recognize that something is off-kilter, but you don't know what to do about it. I'd be a very happy (and chubby) dog if I had a cookie for every time I heard someone say, "Bella's got the best life—she just naps and plays all day." *Ahem, do you think this book just wrote itself?*

DOGS WHO WORK

So how is Bella an expert on the working life? For starters, I am a boxer. According to the dictionary and the American Kennel Club, this makes me a member of the working dog category:

Working Dog (Origin: 1890–95): Any of various breeds of dogs developed or trained to do useful work, such as herding animals, guarding property, performing water rescues and pulling wagons. Quick to learn, working dogs are intelligent, capable animals and make steadfast companions. They include the boxer, bullmastiff, Doberman pinscher, Great Dane, Saint Bernard, Rottweiler and Siberian husky.

OK, so "intelligent," "capable" and "steadfast" are adjectives that I can relate to. As a unique breed, boxers date back to Germany in the late 19th century. During the First and Second World Wars we served as couriers, traveling quietly across enemy territories to carry messages that were attached to our collars. Boxers started gaining popularity in the United States in the late 1930s. Today boxers have a reputation for being excellent police, guardian, therapy and service dogs (not to mention savvy dogpreneurs).

However, when it comes to water rescues, boxers are not exactly the "go to" choice. Most boxers—including me—aren't strong swimmers. Even when I wear the bright yellow life jacket that makes me the laughingstock of Labrador retrievers everywhere, I won't dip more than a few toes into the surf. I can't imagine pulling wagons, either, since the only wagon I know is the Subaru Outback that my humans use to chauffeur me to dog day care and the occasional "yappy hour" (ostensibly for canine socialization but really just another excuse for the two-leggeds to drink half-priced cocktails).

Don't get me wrong, I am not making fun of the work of draft animals or of guide dogs and their search-and-rescue brethren. They are genuine heroes. But there is a new breed of working dog that relies on business savvy and brains. Rather than herd sheep, we're joining the human white-collar workforce. When we're not roaming among cubicles and spreading good cheer, we are climbing the corporate ladder to positions such as Top Dog and Chief Canine Officer.

Work Like a Dog with Your Dog

One out of every five companies across the United States now allows dogs at work, ranging from mom-and-pop shops to large corporations. At the four-star Fairmont Copley Plaza in Boston, for example, the hotel's canine ambassador is a black Labrador named Catie Copley. Catie takes her job seriously, greeting guests upon their arrival to the hotel and accompanying them on scheduled walks and runs. She has her own business cards and e-mail address, and she sends care packages to other dogs staying at the hotel. Managers of the guest services program consider Catie their secret weapon in differentiating the hotel from its competitors.

In Portland, Ore., it's not unusual to hear the patter of paws and claws in the halls of the Portland Opera, where employees are welcome to bring their dogs (and cats) to work. Director Christopher Mattaliano has said that "a happy staff is a productive staff." This is especially true when a new production is in the works and things at opera headquarters get hectic. During these times, pets provide opera employees with much-needed diversion and stress relief and make it easier for them to get back to creating innovative, groundbreaking productions.

In Greensboro, N.C., Replacements Ltd. has the world's largest collection of dinnerware and specializes in replacing broken or missing pieces (a godsend when your dog takes out the china cabinet). Owner Bob Page has been bringing his two dachshunds to work for years and encourages his 500-plus employees—and customers—to bring their pets to the company's offices and showrooms. Company representatives say that no china or crystal has ever been shattered by a dog, although it's a different story with employees and customers.

What if you aren't lucky enough to spend your workdays with your dog? Start small by persuading your boss to roll out the red carpet for your four-legged friend just one day a year. Pet Sitters International started its annual "Take Your Dog to Work Day" (www.takeyourdog.com) in 1999. Thousands of businesses participate each year to celebrate dogs in the workplace and to promote pet adoption.

....

Modern working dogs aren't confined to corporate settings, however. Thanks to technology's ability to connect people from Pasadena to Poughkeepsie, 4.2 million Americans work entirely from home. Another 20 million work from home at least part time. Sitting next to them are their four-legged friends, using the skills they've learned from their humans and becoming dogpreneurs of their own with websites, blogs and online stores.

Dogs have moved from the dog park to the office park, and there are plenty of humans who like it that way. Surveys consistently show that a significant percentage of Americans believe that having a pet in the workplace increases creativity, reduces stress, decreases absenteeism and fosters better relationships among colleagues. In a 2006 poll by Dogster and Simply Hired, 43 percent of dog owners said they would take a 5–10 percent salary reduction if they could bring their dogs to work, and another 55 percent would commute longer distances to work if they could bring their four-legged friends with them. Yet another 66 percent said they would work longer hours with canine companionship, and 49 percent said they would switch employers for a job that allowed dogs.

So what's a little carpet cleaning when dogs have so much to teach their human friends about living successful lives? More important, are people really ready to listen to what a dog has to say, even a savvy dogpreneur like me?

I think so. People do take their dogs seriously. An estimated 1 million dogs in the United States are beneficiaries in their owners' wills. Thirty-three percent of dog owners surveyed admit that they talk to their dogs on the phone or leave them messages on the answering machine. Seventy-seven percent of dog-owning CEOs surveyed say they can judge the character of others based on how they treat dogs and how dogs respond to them.

Clearly, humans value the opinions and feelings of their four-legged friends. Plus I've been successfully dispensing advice to my own humans for the last few years—great advice, just ask them. So here it is: good old-fashioned canine intuition with paws-on work experience to help people achieve success in work and life. The lessons are simple and to the point, complete with my own Bella sound bites, which, to paraphrase Mark Twain, bring "a minimum of sound to a maximum of sense."

With my help you'll live up to your own definition of success while learning to focus on what's important in life and filter out what's not. You'll be happier and more productive, thereby creating extra time to spend with your fuzzy, furry friends.

Life is short, especially in dog years, so go out and unleash your own success!

Chapter 1

Purpose: Discover What Makes You Zoom

Too many men drift lazily into any job, suited or
unsuited for them; and when they don't get along well
they blame everybody and everything but themselves.

– Thomas Edison

He may be a dog, but don't tell me he doesn't
have a real grip on life.

– Kendall Hailey

What makes you zoom? What is it that makes you want
to leap out of bed every morning and go to work? For me,
it's the idea of a brand new day filled with new things to
eat and new people to meet. By the time I gulp down my
last piece of breakfast kibble, I'm charged with excitement
and the "zoomies" hit me. I take off like a rocket, running
circles around the dining room table and skating across

the house on the slippery hardwood floors. Only after all the chairs are knocked over and the rugs are tossed aside do I flop down on my pillow for a well-deserved snooze before I zoom again, right into my day as a working dog.

I think it goes without saying that the zoomies are a whole lot of fun, not to mention a major source of moola for hardwood-floor refinishers. A puppy or dog with a case of the zoomies is releasing pent-up energy and expressing his or her joy and love of life. Thankfully, floors and furniture don't always have to suffer in the process, because exuberance can also take on a quieter tone. A journalist once asked Mahatma Gandhi why he never took a vacation. After working 15 hours a day, every day, for 50 years, Gandhi replied, "I am always on vacation."

Gandhi didn't zip around in circles, but there was no doubt that he had found what made him zoom. His energy, or inner fire, came from living a life that was filled with passion and purpose. Considering how much respect he had for animals, I don't think he'd be offended if I said that he was very "dog-like" in looking at every new day as a gift and an opportunity to discover something new.

CUT TO THE CHASE:
GETTING TO THE HEART OF WHAT'S IMPORTANT

I'm a dog with relatively simple pleasures: eating cheese, chasing balls and sneaking under the bedcovers when my humans leave the house. All my four-legged friends live equally uncomplicated lives. Humans who hear the word "simple" often think of "boring" or "unsophisticated," but that's where they are wrong. Dogs lead simple lives because we don't mess around. We know how to get to the heart of what's important, and we have a knack for helping humans ask themselves how to do the same.

WHAT ENERGIZES YOU
FROM DEEP INSIDE YOUR CORE?

The humans who know me best would say that my core values are empathy, joy and companionship. I agree with them. I'm a dog who loves, loves, loves—insists on, really—being surrounded by happy, positive people. Indeed, I can't imagine any punishment worse than being ignored or left to my own devices. (The same goes for every other boxer I know. If you're thinking about bringing one of us into your family and you can't take us to work with you, take my advice: We are *not* the right breed for you, your fancy furniture or your soon-to-be-shredded landscaping.)

My core values drive me. They are the reason why I consider it my personal mission to give the people around me something to smile about. When I succeed—which is quite often, because I'm very good at what I do—I jump for joy and wiggle my stub tail furiously, like a propeller on a plane about to take off. And when I'm really over the moon, I do the famous boxer "kidney bean" dance, which is me strutting in a U shape so that both my tail and my face are facing the same direction. It takes talent and enthusiasm, and I have both!

My point is that if you want to zoom through life, you need to focus on the things you love and that motivate and energize you from deep inside your core.

So what is that for you?

WHAT'S YOUR PLAN FOR CREATING A MEANINGFUL LIFE?

Dogs are a practical bunch. We know that it's not enough to dream about a satisfying and productive life; it's up to us to make it happen. For example, I want to earn a therapy dog certificate so that I'll be allowed to spread the famous "Bella love" to those who need it the most—patients in hospitals, nursing homes or rehabilitation centers, for example.

So what's the problem? I need to do more than just dream about becoming a therapy dog. I need a plan. Becoming a certified therapy dog is a multistep process that requires time and commitment. This is something that I learned firsthand from my friend Emmi.

Emmi is a sweet rescue pug in southern Nevada who visits patients at the local hospice. She and her two-legged mom began the certification process by studying the legal issues surrounding hospice care and learning all about the needs of patients, their families and the staff. Next, Emmi had to take a practical exam on topics like obedience, following commands, ignoring distractions and interacting with other dogs, people and situations. Finally, Emmi and her mom went on three supervised hospice visits. It took dedication and hard work, but now they are certified to visit the hospice on their own, where they bring love and comfort to patients and their families in very trying times. The moral of Emmi's story is that she and her two-legged mom had a plan and they doggedly stuck with it. They didn't just dream about living a meaningful life, they created one.

What's your plan?

WHAT ARE YOUR STRENGTHS
AND HOW WILL YOU USE THEM?

Unlike my pug pal, Emmi, I'm not a great candidate for hospice work. The size of my paws, the length of my tongue and the springs in my feet (can you say boing, boing?) are a tad overwhelming for people who are elderly, sick or frail. In fact, I'm pretty sure that hospice administrators would not invite me back for a second visit. Does that mean I have to give up on my dream of becoming a therapy dog? Not if I keep working on my manners and look for opportunities to do therapy work with people who can handle my exuberant style, like at-risk teenagers and young adults, for example. And when I start to slow down and get gray whiskers of my own, I may find that I'm qualified to do hospice work.

The one thing that I'm sure of, however, is that I can't change my basic "boxerness." I'll always be an extrovert, sniffing out new friends and giving out as many slobbery dog kisses as possible. Even if I did want to change who I am

13

(which I don't), I know that it's impossible for dogs or humans to create happy and meaningful lives by spending all their time and energy trying to "fix" themselves—whether they need fixing or not. Besides, it's more effective and a lot more fun to concentrate our attention and effort on the things we are good at and that make us feel strong and successful. What we think we can do, we can do.

What would you like to do?

WHO CAN YOU LEARN FROM?

My humans named me Bella after a German shepherd who was a well-loved member of my mom's family. As it turns out, Bella is one of the most popular female dog names of all times, which means that everywhere we go, we run into yet another Bella. But I'm OK with that. My humans reassure me that there is no other dog on the planet quite like me. I'm my very own person, er, dog.

Although individuality is sacred, top dogs also know to look for role models and mentors who have similar qualities and strengths and who've found what makes them zoom. My own personal role model is Zadok, an 81-pound Akita who has traveled nationally as part of a crisis response team assigned to help students deal with the aftermath of the shootings at Virginia Tech and Northern Illinois University. From his breed to his size to his "active greeting style," Zadok is not your typical therapy dog. In fact, his two-legged mom, Julie Burk, didn't begin therapy work with Zadok until he was 4 years old. Even now, at

8, Zadok still needs to manage his energy and enthusiasm, but it hasn't stopped him from being one of the country's top therapy dogs and winning the AKC's Award of Canine Excellence in the therapy division.

Zadok has taught me that there are different ways that I can use my strengths to make other people feel good. Having a strong mentor and guide keeps me motivated and helps me focus on what's important.

Who are your mentors, and why?

HOW TO ZOOM LIKE A HUMAN

There are as many different ways to zoom as there are pets on the planet, whether you're a boxer, a pug or an Akita. The same goes for humans. One such human is Amy Sacks, the founder of the Pixie Project, a nonprofit animal adoption center and retail pet supply store in Portland, Ore. Amy promotes the responsibilities of pet ownership, the importance of spaying and neutering and the positive impacts of pet adoption. Her work offers lessons for others who are trying to find what makes them zoom.

Case Study:
The Pixie Project
....

Amy Sacks' childhood memories include driving around town in a family car that was filled with dog food, treats, toys and bedding. Whenever Amy's mother came across a person living on the street with a companion animal, she would offer to pay for any necessary veterinary care, with the priority being spaying and neutering.

Amy launched her first spay-and-neuter project in college. For guidance, she turned to the president of the local pet shelter, who taught her how to comfort and socialize a shy animal and how to give basic medical care. Amy's mentor also taught her how to avoid becoming overwhelmed by the heartbreak that comes with rescue work. Determined to let people see rescue animals in a positive, uplifting and family-friendly environment and not the stereotypical "sad and depressing" shelter scenario, Amy launched the Pixie Project in 2007. The mission of her bright and airy nonprofit animal adoption center and retail pet supply store is to change the image of rescue, one animal at a time.

The Pixie Project does not accept strays or animals from the public. Instead, it works with high-intake county shelters and takes in loving, family friendly pets whose circumstances have left them in need of a new home. Whereas relationships between rescue groups and crowded county shelters are sometimes strained, the Pixie Project acts an advocate and asset to shelter staff who are often overworked and underfunded.

The Pixie Project has also partnered with Outside In, a local nonprofit that provides job training to at-risk and homeless youth and which runs an on-site day care where adoptable dogs romp alongside family pets. Youth from Outside In staff the day care and also learn retail and customer service skills while working in the Pixie Project's adjacent nonprofit pet supply store.

Since opening, the Pixie Project has found homes for more than 1,000 animals with the help of four staff members and about 50 active volunteers.
www.pixieproject.org

....

Amy didn't just have a passion, she had a plan. With a degree from a prestigious college, she had multiple career options, all of which would have paid far beyond what she earns running a small nonprofit. Yet within a year of her college graduation she outlined her vision for the Pixie Project, got financial backing, found a location, recruited volunteers and set up partnerships with animal shelters and social service agencies. That's because nothing gives Amy the same energy, or inner fire, as animal education and rescue—it's what makes her zoom. "If it takes three hours to counsel a family on the benefits of adoption, I'll gladly spend my time doing so," she says. Amy also had strong mentors and guides. She credits her parents for her sense of social responsibility and for lending their business acumen and financial support to get the Pixie Project off the ground. She is grateful to her first rescue mentor for teaching her how to manage the physical and emotional aspects of working with homeless animals, and she acknowledges that the Pixie Project would not exist without her friend and business partner, Karli Covington.

While Amy acts as the face of the organization, counseling adoptive pet families and managing the nonprofit's public awareness and education programs, Karli "handles everything else that makes our program work." Each partner focuses on her individual strengths: Amy on education and awareness, Karli on management and administration. The result is a stronger, more effective organization whose members are living their core values.

WHEN LIFE THROWS YOU A CURVEBALL

It feels great when everything falls into place and you zoom through life. Unfortunately, even the best-laid plans can come crashing down around you. Whether you have two or four legs, unexpected surprises are an inevitable and unavoidable part of life. Will these curveballs derail you or create fantastic opportunities?

Zooming is great, but sometimes you have to get out of your own way to see new possibilities and to change course. That's what happened to Carol Gardner, whose life took a surprising new direction when she met a wrinkled English bulldog named Zelda.

Case Study:
Zelda Wisdom

Like Amy Sacks, Carol Gardner had a good idea of what she wanted to do when she grew up. As a first-grader she staged a puppet show for which she wrote the script, coordinated the puppets and promoted the event with fliers she passed out in her neighborhood and at school. The puppet show was a huge success, drawing an enthusiastic audience of neighbors, family and friends as well as a columnist from the local newspaper. It also set the stage for a lifetime of creative design work. "I learned to take creativity and run with and have fun with it," says Carol, who enjoyed a successful career in advertising.

Fast-forward to the age of 52, when Carol found herself without any income after the end of her 27-year marriage. "Heartbroken and penniless" is how Carol describes herself back then. Desperate for love and laughter, she found both in Zelda, a fellow under-dog looking for unconditional love. To Carol, looking at Zelda was a bit like looking in a mirror (minus the triple chin, serious underbite and short, stubby tail). Carol says, "We're not perfect, but it's up to each of us to turn our disadvantages into advantages."

Sensing a little bit of Zelda in everyone, Carol en-tered a Christmas card contest sponsored by a lo-cal pet store with a photo of her furry friend in the bathtub wearing a Santa hat and a beard of bubbles. The one-liner read: "For Christmas I got a dog for my husband ... good trade, huh?" Within weeks of win-ning the contest—which came with 40 pounds of free dog food every month for a year—she teamed up with a professional photographer and a publicist and maxed out her credit cards so that she and Zelda would stand apart from the thousand other exhibi-tors at the National Stationery Show. They bet the farm, and it paid off with the launch of Zelda Wisdom and a deal with Hallmark.

Since that first Christmas card, Zelda's sassy sayings have sold millions of greeting cards, books, calendars and gifts around the world. Carol has signed multiple licensing agreements, and she and Zelda have appeared on *Oprah, Good Morning America, The Today Show* and *The Martha Stewart Show,* to name just a few. Zelda is also a "spokesdog" for Delta Society Pet Partners, working with children who have learning disabilities. She and Carol support the Morris Animal Foundation's canine cancer research, the Pet Peace of Mind Program, which cares for pets of the elderly and the terminally ill, and Oregon Dog Rescue. *www.zeldawisdom.com*

....

Clearly, Carol is not afraid to seek out new ways to zoom. The key to her success has been her ability to roll with the punches and reinvent herself accordingly. In her own words, "Life is a puzzle, and the more pieces you make, the bigger and better the picture and the results."

Carol also combines flexibility with a healthy touch of fearlessness. According to her, too many humans never find what makes them zoom because they lack self-confidence. They talk themselves out of opportunities and tell themselves, "I can't do it." Taking her own words of wisdom to heart, Carol has reinvented herself as a public speaker—something she previously feared and now enjoys. Her audiences love her, too. Her speech, "How to Go from Underdog to Top Dog Without Barking Up the Wrong Tree," is a consistent crowd pleaser.

"My life is a vacation," Carol says, echoing the words and wisdom of others who have discovered their passion and purpose in life.

TIME TO REFLECT

I'm a lucky dog and I know it! A few times a year my two-legged humans pack up the station wagon and all my gear, and we vacation in the mountains or at the beach. Although we call these trips "business retreats," we spend a lot of time outdoors swimming, hiking, kayaking or snowshoeing. In the evenings, my humans cook gourmet meals, which they don't have time to make at home. Feeling relaxed, they usually let their "no table scraps rule" lapse—which just adds another great element to my idea of the good life.

People who hear about our adventures say things like "You sure are a pampered pooch" or "When do you ever work?" Fortunately, my humans know that time away from e-mail, phones and the Internet is the best way to recharge and refocus (unlike the third of all American workers who never use the vacation time they've earned). Some of our best ideas, including the one for this book, have come from brainstorming sessions we've had while we've been away from the office.

We also have an annual New Year's Eve tradition where we reflect on our accomplishments and review our business and personal goals for the coming year. It feels good to share our achievements and to talk about ways to turn our dreams into reality in the new year. Since December 31 is also my birthday (which is appropriate, since I love a good party), my humans break out fun hats and dog biscuits and let me unwrap my presents with my teeth.

Although having a free pass to shred paper all over the living room floor is fun, birthday and New Year celebrations also have an uncanny way of putting time into perspective. Things that seemed important six months ago may no longer have meaning, and new opportunities may suddenly appear on the horizon.

Creating a life of passion and purpose is no small feat, but the lesson for humans is that jobs come and go, relationships strengthen and weaken, businesses boom and bust, and today's emergencies are usually meaningless tomorrow (if not, then almost certainly by the end of the week, at least if you're a boxer). Take the time to refresh, reflect and refocus on what's really important.

BELLA'S SOUND BITES

- Concentrate your time and energy on the things that you love and that you are good at—the things that make you "zoom."

- Don't just *dream* about a satisfying and productive life, *create* one. Set goals and create a plan to meet those goals.

- Run with the curveballs that life throws at you. Surprises are inevitable, but they can also lead to fantastic new opportunities.

- Take time to refresh, reflect and refocus on what's really important. You'll live better and work better.

Chapter 2

Body:
Fill Your Lungs,
Stretch Your Limbs

Physical fitness is not only one of the most important
keys to a healthy body, it is the basis of dynamic and
creative intellectual activity.

– John Fitzgerald Kennedy

A dog is one of the remaining reasons why some people
can be persuaded to go for a walk.

– O.A. Battista

Listen up, humans. The way you start the morning has a
huge impact on the rest of your day. You may not realize
it, but your early a.m. antics also affect your dog. How
many of you drag your pooches to the nearest dog park
on the way to work and coax them to "hurry up and go
potty" as you balance a nonfat latté while jabbering on a

cell phone? Seriously, if you can't pay attention to us at the dog park, we'd rather stay home.

Sadly, too many harried humans start their day on autopilot without paying particular attention to what their dogs need, much less what is good for their own bodies and minds. Personally, I don't understand why humans are always in such a rush. Unless someone is buzzing the front doorbell, I don't see the need to catapult out of bed every morning as if the mattress were on fire. It sets a frantic pace that spins out of control as the day goes on and leaves you without anything to show for your efforts. It also explains why your otherwise adoring pet gives you the early morning stank eye.

TAKE A DEEP BREATH

A much better way to start the day is to take a hint from the sleepy-eyed, four-legged creature that has taken over your side of the warm bed: Take a long, deep breath. If you observe how a relaxed dog breathes, you'll see that he or she isn't thinking about yesterday or worrying about tomorrow. Dogs don't care about sucking in their stomachs, either. When you breathe from your diaphragm like you are *supposed* to, your stomach naturally inflates and deflates like a balloon—one more reason to ditch the super-tight skinny jeans. (Besides, how are you going to take your dog on a nice long walk if you don't have any feeling in your legs?)

In contrast to dogs, most humans take short and shallow chest breaths. This is natural in times of great anxiety or immediate danger, like when your boss is yelling at you or a gang of angry Chihuahuas is chasing you down a dark alley. But on an ongoing basis, shallow and rapid breathing can contribute to chronic stress and fatigue. It can also have a negative effect on your mood and leave you feeling tense and grumpy.

The challenge is that breathing is so simple and automatic that people who aren't marathoners or mountain climbers don't usually give it a second thought—even when they're doing it poorly. They breathe in and they breathe out, end of story. Yet slow, deep breathing expands the ribs and delivers oxygen to all the cells of the body while getting rid of carbon dioxide. It slows the heart, clears the head and boosts energy, creativity and physical and emotional well-being. Awareness of breath is also one of the easiest ways to tap into your inner dog and focus on the here and now.

Breathe Like a Dog

Al Lee is an expert in the use of breathing techniques to reduce stress and improve health, performance and emotional well-being. He is a professional speaker and co-author of *Perfect Breathing: Transform Your Life One Breath at a Time*. Al says that dogs are always breathing just the way they need to be, taking full, deep and energizing breaths and dealing with whatever comes their way in the moment, as it comes.

"Dogs don't spend their days hunched over a laptop or behind the steering wheel of a car," notes Al, who admits that the family beagle used to jump behind the wheel whenever given the chance. "And generally speaking, dogs don't spend their evenings slumped in an easy chair watching *Real Housewives of New Jersey*." (Plus, I don't understand why humans would want to watch that drivel in the first place.)

Al wisely observes that dogs don't bottle up stress and hold their breath when they are stuck in traffic. Moreover, dogs don't hyperventilate rehashing last week's trip to the veterinarian, and they don't fume or wallow in the fight-or-flight response for hours after a dustup at the dog park. Humans, on the other hand, have developed the bad habit of taking short and shallow breaths into the top of their lungs. Thanks to all the stress that comes with modern lifestyles, most humans have "forgotten" how to breathe properly. Only by developing awareness of their breath do people notice when it begins to change—which is almost always when they replay the past or worry about the future.

"Dogs know that nothing happens in the past or the future," says Al. "Life is only now, in this moment. By 'breathing like a dog,' we become fully present to *what* is happening, *when* it's happening."

To begin the day in a calm, relaxed and present state of mind, take five minutes to concentrate on your breathing:

- Close your eyes.
- Inhale from your belly for three seconds and pause briefly.

- Exhale from your belly for three seconds and pause.
- Repeat as necessary.

To make it a habit, try taking a cue from your dog: Every time he or she lets out a satisfied sigh, straighten your posture and focus on your breathing. Soon it will become a natural part of your daily routine.

Visit *www.perfectbreathing.com* for more breathing exercises.

STRETCH YOUR LIMBS

Personally, I like to practice my deep breathing exercises around 5:30 a.m., within earshot of my still-asleep humans. When I've made sure that everyone is wide awake, I continue my morning routine with a few calisthenics on the bedroom floor. First I arch my back. Next I stick out my forepaws and take a bow. Then I pump out my chest, stretch my back legs out as far as they can go and pretend to fly through the sky like Underdog. By the time I'm finished, even my stubby little boxer tail feels energized.

Regrettably, there are plenty of humans who think that stretching is boring or painful. This is true if your idea of stretching is hanging over your knees and bouncing up and down trying to grab your toes. But stretching done right improves circulation, releases tension and builds strength, energy and flexibility, which is why dogs stretch throughout the day (plus it's fun). Anyone who scrunches over a desk, computer or steering wheel knows that it's hard to enjoy the here and now when their legs, neck, back, shoulders and wrists are stiff and achy. Stretching releases that tension and shifts the focus back to the present.

Stretching also reminds the body how good it feels to get up and move. Let's face it: Since dogs and humans started hanging out more than 12,000 years ago, we've all gotten more sedentary. The result is that one-third of adult humans in the United States are obese, and more than 44 percent of dogs are either overweight or obese. This puts both species at greater risk for injury and raises the risk of heart disease, diabetes, cancer, arthritis and depression.

Dogs weren't bred to spend 18 hours a day napping, and humans weren't designed to sit on their backsides for hours at a time. According to Dr. James Levine of the Mayo Clinic in Minnesota, today's humans suffer from "sitting disease," and burn anywhere from 1,500 to 2,000 fewer calories per day than they did just 30 years ago. Stretching is an excellent way to teach the body to start moving again. It circulates feel-good hormones up to the brain and can even be the catalyst for a brand new exercise program.

Exercise: **Good Doga**

Yoga for humans and dogs, or doga, is the latest way to spend quality time together. Fortunately, you don't need a yoga mat, fancy yoga pants or even a dog to stretch your body gently and to relieve stress and fatigue.

Adho mukha svanasana, or downward-facing dog, is a pose that stretches the whole body and increases blood flow to the brain, which helps with memory and concentration. It builds upper-body strength and releases the tightness in the hips and hamstrings that leads to back pain. Best of all, you can do downward-facing dog any time of the day—just remember to remove your collar and dog tags, as they get in the way and make annoying clanking noises. Here's how:

- Get down on the floor on your hands and knees, palms spread, wrists underneath your shoulders and knees underneath your hips.

- Pressing firmly through your hands, exhale and lift your knees off the floor. At first keep the knees slightly bent while straightening your legs and lengthening your tailbone. Slowly stretch your heels down toward the floor. Don't lock your knees.

- Walk your hands forward a few inches to lengthen the pose, but keep your head relaxed and move your shoulder blades away from your ears toward your hips. Focus your gaze between your feet.

- Hold the position as long as it is comfortable.

When you are finished, sink into *Balasana*, or child's pose. Bring your knees to the floor and rest your hips on your heels and your forehead on the floor. You can stretch your arms in front of you with your palms toward the floor or bring them alongside your body with your palms facing upward. Child's pose is restful and relaxing—unless you happen to have a four-legged friend who wedges herself onto your yoga mat and demands a belly rub. (Of course, I don't personally know such a dog, but I recommend giving in to the belly rub. It's good for your dog and it's great for your spirit!)

WALK IT OFF

I'll admit, there are some days when all I want to do is indulge my inner canine couch potato (especially after I've convinced my humans that I should be allowed to sit on the living room couch). But nothing rouses me from a deep slumber like someone dangling a leash in front of my nose and saying, "Let's go for a walk."

Walking is one of the easiest ways for both dogs and humans to get into shape. With just a little bit of leash training, dogs make excellent walking partners, too. That's because we're supportive, nonjudgmental and dependable. We don't care where you are going, what you are wearing or what kind of shape you are in—we're just happy to tag along and keep you company. (Well, if you keep us all safe. Walking a black Labrador in the pre-dawn hours while dressed in black like a Ninja is just plain dumb and happens all the time in my neighborhood. Spend a few dollars and buy proper reflective gear for both you and your fur baby so that people, especially drivers, can see you no matter what the weather or time of day.)

Dogs are also quite persuasive when it comes to nudging our humans off their backsides and out the front door. If you have an excuse, we have a counterpoint:

Human: *I'm too tired.*

Dog: *Just take me out for 15 minutes of fresh air—you want me to have fresh air, right?—and then I promise we can go back inside unless you suddenly find the energy to keep going (which, of course, you will).*

•••••

Human: *Walks are boring.*

Dog: *OK, I'll make it interesting. I'll dawdle to sniff a blade of grass and then I'll take off running after a squirrel. It's called interval training, and I'll be your own personal trainer.*

•••••

Human: *Sorry, I forgot—things got really busy today.*

Dog: *Pick a time of day and put it on your calendar. I promise to remind you daily by thumping my tail on the floor, barking at the door and/or yanking your computer cord out of the wall. Walking will become a new habit in no time.*

•••••

Human: *I don't feel like it.*

Dog: *Here's the deal. I don't feel like dressing up for Halloween, but I do it because I love you and it makes you and all your YouTube friends crack up. Now lace up your sneakers and let's go.*

"What if I don't have a dog?" you ask. Well, borrow a dog or find a loaner dog by volunteering to exercise a neighbor's pet or to walk dogs at the local animal shelter. Most shelters desperately need people who can give dogs the physical activity they need to stay healthy, happy and adoptable.

You're not just making a dog's life better, you'll also be improving your own health and fitness. Researchers in England found that people with dogs exercised up to six hours more per week than people who worked out on their own or in a gym, and a study by the University of Missouri showed that new walkers who were matched with loaner dogs and walked just 20 minutes a day for five days a week lost an average of 14 pounds over the course of a year.

If you still can't find a dog, then grab the next best thing: a human friend, relative, neighbor or co-worker. Just don't try walking with a cat. Research shows that the key to sticking with a workout program is having the support and encouragement of a regular exercise partner, someone who is equally motivated to make a change—and not some fickle feline who'll wander any way the wind blows (or not at all).

If you think you don't have time to exercise, consider that it can make you *more* efficient than ever by boosting your concentration, energy and productivity. Look to us dogs for proof: We are tangible, butt-wiggling reminders that regular physical activity is a basic and instinctual animal need. With enough exercise, dogs are happy, relaxed and confident. Without it, we're anxious, stressed and bored. Humans are no different. So the next time you need to blow off some steam, be like a dog and go for a walk, jog or run. You may be surprised by how much fun it is and how good it makes you feel.

Case Study:
Thank Dog! Bootcamp

A four-legged workout partner can be just the motivation that humans need to get out the door and into shape. Jill and Jamie Bowers, twin sisters and certified dog trainers, started Thank Dog! Bootcamp in southern California in 2008 as a way for humans to lose weight and tone up while providing their dogs with exercise and obedience training. They even created a "Borrow-A-Dog" program for people who don't have a dog of their own.

Jill developed the concept after losing 40 pounds in a "traditional" (i.e., human-only) boot camp program. She thought, "Why not create a workout that lets people partner with their dogs?" The result is an hour-long outdoor fitness program that combines cardiovascular and strength training for humans with obedience training for dogs. Participants get into shape while saving money on extra fees like gym memberships, personal trainers, dog walkers and obedience classes. "Many of our members have already reached their fitness goals," says Jill. "But they keep coming five days a week because they're having fun and because they go home with a well-trained, happy and tired dog."

The dogs aren't the only ones who are being trained, however. Jill and Jamie know that people who work out with their four-legged friends are more likely to make exercise a consistent part of their daily routine. "Dogs are creatures of habit," says Jill. "They get into routines, and their humans feel responsible for maintaining those routines. Once they get into a groove and start seeing results, humans start to look forward to exercising as much as their dogs do."
www.thankdogbootcamp.com

As certified dog trainers, Jill and Jamie also emphasize the importance of staying patient and positive to keep a dog from associating a session with a negative experience. The same holds true for humans and exercise. If you expect to master a new sport on the first attempt, or try to lose 10 pounds in a single week, you will be frustrated.

The lesson for dogs and humans is the same: Acknowledge small accomplishments and successes along the way, and make sure that you end every workout on a positive note—it's the only surefire way to make exercise feel like fun.

A FINAL THOUGHT

As great as exercise is (really!), there are those cold winter days when I'd rather curl up next to the heating vent than go jogging through the city streets tethered to my humans. Yet once I start moving, nothing beats the euphoria that comes with feeling healthy and strong. This same feeling is what motivates my two-legged mom to drag herself out of bed for early morning workout classes at the local health club. Another reason is the positive energy of her instructor, Jenny Walker.

Jenny ends every class by reminding her sweat-soaked students that they should feel a sense of gratitude—gratitude for having the skill, ability and good health to work out when there are millions of people who would give anything for the chance to exercise but cannot because of illness or injury. "It's amazing the response I get from the people who take my exercise classes," Jenny says. "If I get distracted and forget to do the 'gratitude saying,' my students let me hear about it!"

Jenny provides an excellent reminder for us to use our bodies to their full capabilities and be grateful for all that they can do. Still not convinced? If you can't (or won't) take care of your body for your own sake, then do it for the sake of your four-legged friends. Think pets can't inspire significant human change? Consider the survey of 3,300 pet owners in which nearly one in three smokers said the health of a family pet would motivate them to try to kick the habit. Think about it: Smokers who aren't willing to quit for the sake of their own health would make significant changes after finding out that secondhand smoke poses a health threat to their pets. Inspired yet? I am, and I'm a dog!

So, grab a leash and go exercise with your dog. You'll make your loyal friend very happy and add quality time to his life—and to yours.

BELLA'S SOUND BITES

- Create a regular routine in which you take a few moments every day to pay attention to what your body needs.

- Be aware of your breath. You'll feel calmer, have more energy and accomplish more than you thought was possible.

- Make time for physical exercise. It will keep you healthy, happy and balanced—and make you appreciate all the amazing things that your body can do.

- Celebrate small victories. Your dog doesn't expect you to change your habits overnight, and neither should you.

Chapter 3

Attitude:
Make Happiness
Happen

Happiness is an attitude. We either make ourselves
miserable, or happy and strong. The amount
of work is the same.

– Francesca Reigler

It's a sorry dog that won't wag its own tail.

– Former U.S. Attorney General Griffin Bell

Dogs wake up every morning just excited to be alive.
It doesn't matter where they've spent the night, either.
I should know, too, because thousands of lucky dogs
around the country curl up with their two-legged companions for the night, but I sleep on a pillow on the floor.
Why? My coldhearted humans refuse to let me sleep
in their bed—a serious injustice, considering that they

sprawl on a California king, the granddaddy of all mattresses. Honestly, how much space can one petite, well-mannered boxer occupy?

On the bright side, it's impossible to wake up on the wrong side of the bed if you aren't sleeping in one in the first place. And since every new day holds the promise of adventure (or at least the chance to score some favorite treats), I get up as early as I can to share my joy with my humans by nudging them out of their comfortable slumber with my cold, wet nose.

For content canines like me there's no such thing as the Sunday night "blues" or the Monday morning "blahs." Every single day is another chance to be happy. Especially a workday, since I'm a dogpreneur with attitude—the good kind, of course.

AS HAPPY AS YOU CHOOSE

Aside from dogs, who are the happiest creatures in the world? The answer: those who make it their business to be happy. As Abraham Lincoln once said, "Most people are about as happy as they make up their minds to be." Recent research backs him up, too. Psychologists have found that half of a human's predisposition to happiness is genetic, but the other half is entirely within his or her own control.

Rick Foster and Greg Hicks, authors of *How We Choose to Be Happy: The 9 Choices of Extremely Happy People—Their Secrets, Their Stories*, agree with Abraham Lincoln. However, unlike the 16th president of the United States, whose beloved companion was a floppy-eared mixed breed named Fido, neither Rick nor Greg has a four-legged partner, thanks to a grueling travel schedule that has taken them to all seven continents. Along the way, they've talked to thousands of people and learned that the happiest and most productive creatures on Earth are those who make a conscious effort to focus on the positive, no matter how small or seemingly inconsequential.

"Regardless of language, geography or cultural traditions, many of the happiest people on Earth *make it their job* to feel joyful," explains Rick. "In other words, they think in advance about how they'd like to think and how they'd like to react. They set their intention to be happy instead of leaving it to chance."

Because the human brain is most receptive to internal programming first thing in the morning, Rick and Greg suggest that people generate excitement and purpose for the day ahead by setting their intentions before they even get out of bed. A statement of intention can be a general statement ("I'm going to do everything I can today to make this a happy, productive and fun day") or it can be specific ("I'm going to express appreciation to Bella today for being the greatest dog ever").

Of course, setting an intention works any time of the day. It's particularly helpful before a meeting or an event, especially one that might be as stressful or difficult as a trip to the veterinarian or an encounter with the dog park bully, for example. It's a powerful way to send a message about who you want to be, how you want to react and what actions you want to take—all of which play into the event's outcome and leave you well equipped to deal with life's inevitable roadblocks and frustrations.

"It's the closest thing to a time machine we know," Rick says. "You can shape the future if you take a minute to set your intention before going into any situation."

THE POWER OF PAWSITIVE THINKING

A dog is what a dog thinks. Every time I strut into the park assuming that everyone wants to be my friend, I leave it with a brand new group of friends. That's because dogs knew about and understood the "Law of Dogtraction" long before humans turned their own version into the subject of mega-selling books and videos.

The principle is simple: You attract into your life the things you think about. This doesn't mean that I can stare at a jar of peanut butter and make it fly off the kitchen counter and into my wide-open and eagerly awaiting jaws (no matter how often I try). I also don't sit around willing my humans to take me to the park. Instead, I visualize how much fun we'll have there, and then I do whatever it takes to turn those pictures in my head into reality— whether it's bouncing a tennis ball at their feet, pacing in circles around their desks or howling loudly at the front door while wearing my most soulful expression. The thing is, I never consider the possibility of *not* going to the park. I don't waste time thinking about all the lame excuses that my humans might come up with. Why? Because in my mind I'm already sprinting across the park's freshly manicured lawns. It's a lot easier to turn focused, positive thoughts into action when you haven't already put up imaginary roadblocks in your head.

With all of this said, however, I'm also a dog—so I know that reality sometimes bites and that I just have to deal with it. Sure, I believe in silver linings, but I also live with real humans in the real world. No matter what the positive-thinking gurus say, the idea that a positive and cheerful attitude alone can make everything better is a recipe for disappointment.

The truth is that the problems of the animal world and the human world are gigantic. Sometimes, they make it difficult for anyone, dog or human, to feel like they can make a difference. The "big picture" can be so overwhelming that it makes a sensitive dog like me want to run to the backyard, dig a hole and bury her head.

So what's the secret to staying motivated when things get tough? Dog kibble. Yes, take small, kibble-sized bites to tackle a complex issue or challenge without becoming overwhelmed. Focus on things that you can do yourself *right here and right now*, no matter how small.

Case Study:
Freekibble.com

....

Mimi Ausland of Bend, Ore., has been volunteering at the Humane Society of Central Oregon since she was 7. After seeing firsthand how hard it is for shelters to get donations of food, Mimi decided to do something more. She decided to help feed the dogs at her local pet shelter.

Inspired by an online vocabulary game that donates rice to the UN World Food Program, Mimi enlisted her parents' help to design a website and recruited a local pet store to supply food. And she made her website fun by offering a "Bow Wow Trivia Game." Visitors could answer a different trivia question every day, and whether the answer was right or wrong, the site would donate 10 pieces of kibble to the shelter.

With all the pieces in place, Mimi launched *Freekibble.com* on April 1, 2008. Amazingly, the 11-year-old collected more than 170,000 pieces of kibble in the first month.

Word of Mimi's success spread quickly. The bubbly young activist was featured in newspapers and magazines across the country, and she chatted with Ellen DeGeneres and Oprah Winfrey on their television shows. Despite the celebrity attention, Mimi remained focused on helping homeless animals and launched a second site, *Freekibblekat.com*, to collect food for shelter cats.

To date, Mimi and *Freekibble.com* and *Freekibble kat.com* (together with their generous sponsors) have donated more than 3.7 million meals of good, healthy dog and cat kibble to over 90 shelters, rescue groups and food banks, and they expect to extend the program in the future.

www.freekibble.com, www.freekibblekat.com

Mimi Ausland demonstrates how a single, positive change can quickly set in motion a chain of events that make the world a much better place. As her programs continue to expand, Mimi still personally delivers free kibble to her local animal shelter, where she volunteers several hours per week while attending middle school, answering e-mails and helping her father create trivia questions for the websites.

Sometimes it's a bit overwhelming. "I definitely have my moments," admits Mimi. "But animals have such a nice, positive attitude and they give back so much joy. They always give me energy." Mimi also gets a kick out of seeing the influence she's had on her peers: "All my friends have started volunteering at the shelter and most of the kids in my class, too!" Mimi's dream is to someday run an animal sanctuary. Judging from her positive, "can do" attitude, she is certain to turn that dream into a reality. And it all started with a few pieces of kibble.

GETTING TO THE HEART OF HUMOR

Humans are constantly debating whether dogs have a sense of humor. Let me put it this way: If we didn't, we wouldn't be able to put up with you. A dog will laugh at anything and anyone, including him- or herself, because life is much too short to be uptight, most creatures are ridiculously funny whether they mean to be or not, and nobody wants to hang around a sourpuss.

If you need further proof that dogs have a sense of humor, just pick up a copy of *DogJoy: The Happiest Dogs in the Universe.* The book features 400 photos that were submitted to editors of *The Bark* magazine for its popular "Smiling Dogs" column. It proves once and for all that dogs not only smile but also giggle, grin, snicker and snort with happiness.

Like hot dogs and cheese (two of my favorite foods), humor and a positive attitude go hand in hand, or paw in hand, as the case may be. It's hard to be negative or depressed and laugh at the same time—so why don't humans laugh more often? One explanation is the speed of life. Humans eat in quick-serve restaurants, get their oil changed at quick-lube shops and are fascinated with television shows about quick home makeovers. Unfortunately, when life doesn't go exactly as planned, they are also quick to become disappointed or angry. They can't (or won't) see the humor in a negative or less-than-ideal situation until the situation is over and done with—if then.

According to motivational humorist Gail Hand, the challenge for humans is to learn how to get to humor *faster* and *more often.* A former stand-up comedian, Gail teaches corporations, universities and associations about the power of laughter, even with serious subjects like alcohol and drug awareness or stress management. When she delivers a presentation, Gail makes her audience laugh by interjecting silly photos of her four dogs, Desi, Lucy, Zippy and Zoe.

"The instant the dogs appear on-screen," says Gail, "people start chuckling. There's just something funny about showing a pair of Chihuahuas and a pair of shih tzus that makes even people who don't consider themselves 'dog people' start laughing."

Gail uses her dogs to teach people to look for the humorous elements of a situation right away, before anger or frustration can take hold. When people feel tired, stressed out and preoccupied with the "crisis du jour," Gail says, they should "pretend that they have to sit down and explain the whole situation to their dog." Suddenly, things don't seem quite so upsetting. They may even seem preposterous.

Case Study:
The Cheezburger Empire

Speaking of preposterous, I can't think of anything more absurd than a bunch of wacky cats speaking kitty pidgin ("oh hai, the itteh bitty kittehs r coming to giv u sum luv"). And yet my two-legged mom logs on to the *I Can Has Cheezburger* website a dozen times a day.

So what gives? Apparently, humans needing a bit of levity in their lives have discovered that pets can make them laugh in cyberspace as well as in real life. As a result, the *I Can Has Cheezburger* site has had more than 1 billion page views in less than three years, making it one of the most popular websites of all time.

"Nothing makes my day more than finding the next funny Internet hit that will make millions of people just a bit happier," says Ben Huh, CEO of Seattle-based Cheezburger Network. Ben's mission is to make people happy for five minutes each day, and with dozens of websites that let people share what they find funny, his media company offers something for every sense of humor (which still doesn't adequately explain why Mom thinks the cats on *I Can Has Cheezburger* are way funnier than the dogs on *I Has a Hot Dog*, but whatever).

Ben's own inspiration for happiness comes from Nemo, a 12-year-old poodle–bichon frise mix adopted from a shelter. "Nemo always looks depressed," says Ben, "but he brings a ton of joy into our lives. He focuses on just a few things that he loves: us, the ball and food. How much more do you need in life?"

Nemo's simple, less-is-more approach to life may explain why the websites in the Cheezburger Network appear basic, even amateurish. This is, of course, an essential part of their genius and charm. Naturally, cats and dogs don't need any extra props to be funny. They have an uncanny ability to help humans see humor in the most unlikely places—and there is certainly nothing cheez-y about that!

www.cheezburger.com

SHAKE OFF NEGATIVITY

A few years ago, I started putting on the pounds. Much to my chagrin, my humans started rationing my food, and soon I slimmed back down to the svelte boxer you see in this book. Similarly, when my dad discovered that his rich media diet was pumping him up with negativity, he vowed to cut back on his consumption. He stopped listening to the radio in the morning. He canceled his subscription to cable television. He limited the amount of time he spent surfing the Internet. As a result, he went from a self-described news junkie to a happier, more productive person with extra time to spend with the people (and dog) he loves.

Now, I'm all for being an informed, educated and involved citizen of the world. But too many humans like my dad gorge on a media diet that saps their time and makes it hard to maintain a positive outlook on life. Sadly, the press has discovered that reporting on scary or depressing news is a formula for attracting a large audience. An "if it bleeds, it leads" mentality guarantees that a good chunk of what you see, hear and read paints an unnecessarily grim, unbalanced view of the world. Since the media serves as one big echo chamber, we all end up hearing the same soul-sucking stories over and over again.

So what is a media-saturated human to do? Start by shaking off salacious and sensational headlines like a dog in the bathtub shakes off water. You may not be able to avoid negativity, but you don't have to absorb it, either. It's as easy to fill your head with positive things as it is to fill it with garbage, so why not focus on the positive? My mom justifies her own daily Cheezburger habit as a way to balance the nonstop scrolling headlines about gossip, crime and global meltdown. Judging from the success of Ben Huh's media empire, she's not alone. There are plenty of other humans just as smart—and positive—as she is.

DON'T BARK BACK

Last but not least, dogs—and all four-legged creatures for that matter—are able to deflect negativity because we don't take things personally. We don't spend precious time obsessing over whether things are "fair" or "unfair." They just are. Dog meets obstacle. Dog jumps over obstacle. End of story.

I'm trying to teach my own two-legged humans these lessons, and they seem to be catching on. For instance, my dad came out of a shop to find that a woman had parked her car too close to his. As he tried to squeeze behind the wheel, his door brushed hers and she exploded. I mean, sheesh, there was no harm done. The car wasn't scratched and nobody peed on it, for goodness' sake. So why did she get so mad?

When my dad realized that the situation was about her and not about him, he saw it for what it was: ridiculous. Wisely, he decided not to respond. Clearly, someone who goes red in the face and spits out an obscenity-laced string of insults while white-knuckling a frothy coffee drink can either ruin your day or give you something to laugh about for weeks. It's your choice. No stewing, no resentment, no grudges—and no barking back. By refusing to let people dump their unhappiness on you, and by not taking every little thing as a personal affront, you deflect needless, negative energy.

BELLA'S SOUND BITES

- Set your intention to be happy by concentrating on the positive, no matter how small or inconsequential it seems.

- Practice the "law of dogtraction" through focused, constructive thoughts.

- Concentrate on the things that you can do right here and right now. One positive change can quickly lead to another.

- Look for the elements of humor in every situation, before anger or frustration grab you by the scruff of the neck.

Chapter 4

Focus:
Keep Your Eyes
on the Ball

Nothing can add more power to your life than
concentrating all of your energies on a
limited set of targets.

— Nido Qubein

If you think dogs can't count, try putting three
dog biscuits in your pocket and then giving
Fido only two of them.

— Phil Pastoret

Concentration is hard work. Dogs are good at it. Humans aren't.

To see concentration personified (or rather, dogified), observe a pointer at work. Pointers are hunting dogs who freeze in their tracks and let a hunter know there is a bird nearby by pointing or crouching. They stay completely motionless until the hunter gets into position and gives the next command.

Although I admire the dogged discipline of a pointer, I personally don't care much for quail, grouse or anything that has a sharp beak or a set of razor-like talons. Instead, I prefer to focus on my little rubber ball. It is often the object of my full and devoted attention (and, dare I say it—love). I stop dead in my tracks as soon as I see it, and I'd be happy to stalk and retrieve the ball all day long if it didn't drive my officemates to the brink of insanity.

Of course, hunting dogs and obsessive-compulsive boxers don't demonstrate such fierce concentration in everything they do. We'd get exhausted! But here's the lesson: Focus on the few things that are most important to you— give them your full attention, energy and talent—and you'll have a job well done plus feel an invigorating sense of satisfaction.

TOO TIRED TO THINK

So why do humans have trouble focusing? For starters, they're too tired to think. The Centers for Disease Control and Prevention estimates that as many as 70 million Americans suffer from sleep disorders or constant sleep loss. I'm chagrined to report that pets don't help in this regard, as sharing a bed with a furry housemate is cited as a leading cause of insomnia. There goes that hope I had of being allowed to sleep on the bed.

Unfortunately, dogs haven't been able to persuade their humans who are "dog tired" (another misnomer) to embrace the concept of power napping, despite evidence that naps improve mental alertness, boost productivity, reduce stress and lower the risk of heart attacks. Some people think that napping is a sign of weakness or laziness, but I think that famous nappers like Albert Einstein, Winston Churchill and Bill Clinton would disagree. Moreover, new research shows that high-income earners are likely to take naps during the day.

Exercise: The Perfect Power Nap

I have no idea why the word "catnap" describes a short, sweet snooze, whereas the word "dognap" brings up images of Cruella de Vil. Nevertheless, dogs and cats know very well that catching a few zzzzzz's during the day is a way to rest and refresh the body and the mind. Here's how:

- Embrace the nap. Dogs don't make excuses for napping, and neither should you. Don't try to "steal a few winks" or get "caught napping." Be a proud napper—there's nothing to be ashamed of!

- Listen to your body. Biologically, most humans feel their energy dip about eight hours after they've gotten out of bed, which makes early afternoon an ideal time to take a snooze. Scientists say that a 20–45-minute power nap anywhere from 1 to 3 p.m. is just what the body and brain need for a burst of energy and creative ideas.

- Create a nap zone. I like to drag my dog pillow to the nearest sun puddle, where I fluff and fold it a dozen times before I finally curl up into a ball and settle down. Find what's comfortable for you— preferably a place where you can lie down and stretch out (research says that it takes 50 percent longer to fall asleep when you are sitting upright).

- Calm your body and mind. Use the breathing techniques described in Chapter 2 and get your body ready for sleep by relaxing your eyes, jaws and body. Let go of the thoughts that scurry through your mind like squirrels. I find it helpful to think about running on a long sandy beach, where there are no squirrels. When it's time to wake up, open your eyes slowly and take a few more deep breaths while stretching your limbs.

Feeling good now? Then go wake up your drooling, snoring and nap-happy dog for a well-deserved play session before getting back to work.

....

THE MYTH OF MULTITASKING

Another reason humans can't concentrate: They are slaves to time. Tyrannical little clocks, watches and PDAs manage every minute of their waking lives. My own humans are guilty of running around in a frenzy while using tired phrases like "There's no time," "Time's up" or "Maybe another time" (which really means "I can't play fetch with you right now because I have a hundred other things to do so please quit dropping your slobbery little red rubber ball into my lap").

We all have the same 24 hours a day to work (and play) with, yet time doesn't have the same grip on dogs as it does on our two-legged companions. (Indeed, the concepts of "minute" and "hour" don't exist for us, so reassuring your fur baby that you'll be back in "five minutes" has no calming effect whatsoever—he just knows you're leaving without him, and he's not very happy about it.) The result is that humans try to cram as much as possible into the time they have. In the process, they've turned multitasking into a badge of honor—even though it's impossible to do many things at once and do any of them well. Brains simply aren't wired this way. Plus, the constant switching between tasks can be as frustrating and as unproductive as doing nothing at all.

Case Study:
Lessons from Sinatra
....

Marci Alboher writes and speaks on career and workplace trends. Her book, *One Person/Multiple Careers: A New Model for Work/Life Success*, popularized the term "slash" to describe people who define themselves through multiple roles instead of a single job title. For example, I have a friend who is a dog walker/archaeologist/entrepreneur. I can't vouch for her other skills, but she's a dog walker extraordinaire.

Marci shares an office with Sinatra, her French bulldog. Sinatra has changed the way that Marci works, lives and multitasks. She wrote about the experience in her "Shifting Careers" blog for *The New York Times* (which is, incidentally, how I reached out to Marci and found out that she has a soft spot for cute boxers).

One of the first things that Sinatra taught Marci on their daily walks through New York City is that multi-tasking can cause bodily harm. Nationwide, trips to the emergency room have skyrocketed as people try to walk, talk, text and even drive at the same time. Since it's impossible to both read e-mail on your cell and keep a curious dog from eating sidewalk scum, Marci wisely leaves her cell at home when she and Sinatra go out.

Multitasking can also lead to a sense of desperation, which Marci describes as a day of toggling between computer windows, chasing down online links, and taking multiple breaks to check e-mail or Twitter. At the end of such a day, with 20 or 30 computer windows open, it's frustrating to have a virtual "to-do" list that isn't any closer to being "done" than it was in the morning.

But multitasking isn't confined to cell phones or laptops. Marci describes her busy morning routine in which she makes tea, pays bills, listens to the news and fixes Sinatra's food and her own cereal at the same time. In Marci's words, "I'm waiting for the day the dog's kibble ends up in my cereal bowl."

Fortunately, Sinatra doesn't seem to mind Marci's multitasking. For him, it's all in a day's work, considering that his job title is best friend/mentor/time-management guru. Nonetheless, he serves as a living, breathing reminder of how important it is to focus. Whenever Sinatra's kibble almost ends up in her cereal bowl, Marci knows it's time to push small and urgent tasks to the background so she can complete an article, finish a project or simply spend time with Sinatra. *www.heymarci.com*

The message to humans from Sinatra, and all dogs, is simple: You think you can do it all, but you can't. Stop classifying everything as "high priority." Only then will you have more time to figure out what's really a priority and what can wait until tomorrow, next week, next year—or maybe never.

COMMANDING ATTENTION

One of the first commands that most puppies hear is "leave it." Trainers agree that "leave it" is important because it teaches dogs to ignore distractions and helps keep them out of trouble. Since I liked to chew on anything from rocks to cigarette butts to rosebuds, it was a command that I heard quite often as a youngster. (Compared with my best friend, Norman, however, I was an angel. A very handsome chocolate Labrador with an affinity for underwear, Norman landed in the emergency animal hospital so many times as a puppy that the intake technicians would greet his humans with "What is it this time, bikinis or briefs?")

The point is that good commands, or good rules, can help keep us on the right track. Since concentration is a skill to be developed and improved, I've come up with a few of my own commands to help humans sharpen their focus and manage their time.

Command #1: Plan Your Day

Ever wonder where "the tail that wags the dog" came from? Well, just start your day without a plan of action and you'll quickly find out what it means. It doesn't take long to get sidetracked by all of life's small distractions. Before you know it, you are chasing the neighbor's cat or chewing on a pair of expensive Italian leather sandals. Meanwhile, important and life-changing projects—such as writing a book on what it takes to succeed in work and life—never get off the ground.

The solution is to prioritize the things you need to do and create a daily action plan. Unlike the tired old "to-do" list, which implies a laundry list of errands, an action plan is what it sounds like—a plan that is filled with action. It's ambitious; it breaks tasks down into manageable steps (e.g., write a page instead of a chapter, teach your dog one new command instead of 10); and it emphasizes progress and results.

I'm not saying that a daily action plan can't include tasks such as "pick up dry cleaning" and "buy dog food" (very important), but it should remind you to tackle your most important tasks first. It should also help you identify and get rid of the things you do out of habit, a sense of obligation or because you just can't say no. Of course, all work and no play make for a very dull human—so include some fun stuff, too. It can be as simple as reading a magazine, going to the gym or enjoying a long walk on the beach with your four-legged friend.

A full schedule doesn't have to be stressful if it keeps you motivated and helps you stop wasting time and stay focused. As the saying goes, "if you want something done, ask a busy person (or dog)."

Command #2: Dump the Distractions

Why do dog trainers tell new puppy parents to pick up their socks and underwear? It's simple: If it's in plain sight, it's fair game. (Here's a gruesome fact: According to Veterinary Pet Insurance Company, socks and underwear are the two most common surgically removed items from pets.) But humans are easily distracted, and they forget. And distractions are everywhere.

If you are addicted to e-mail, turn it off. If gossip headlines are your Achilles' heel, close your Internet browser. If you can't let a ringing phone go unanswered, pull the plug. Right now you are saying, "Easier said than done." Yes, dogs, especially successful dogpreneurs, know firsthand that removing temptation takes a lot of hard work and self-discipline. For instance, to focus on finishing this book, I had to put away my red rubber ball. (Well, the truth is that I accidentally wedged it underneath the sofa, where it remains solidly stuck. The result, however, is the same. Distraction gone! At least until one of my humans retrieves it for me.)

If you are one of those people who lose focus and don't know why, start taking notes—write down everything you do during your workday. You will quickly learn that you create your own distractions by making a telephone call or opening your inbox to send "just one more" e-mail. Maybe you procrastinate by dropping by a colleague's desk—and now there are two of you who are distracted. Like dieters who keep food journals, time wasters are more likely to change their ways when they see evidence of their bad habits in black and white.

Here's another idea. For people and dogs who like round, shiny red objects, Francesco Cirillo created a time-management method called the Pomodoro Technique that uses a basic red tomato kitchen timer to break tasks into 25-minute increments called "pomodoros," which means "tomatoes" in Italian. Boy, do I love tomatoes. Especially the little cherry tomatoes that come straight off the vine ... but I digress. The goal of the technique is to keep you focused and working in increments, one pomodoro at a time, until a task is completed. At the same time, you keep track of every single interruption on a sheet of paper so that you can eliminate them over time. It's simple and clever, and there's even a free instructional booklet at *www.pomodorotechnique.com*.

Command #3: Finish What You Start

Boxer people know that if you interrupt a boxer while she's digging a hole, she'll whine and obsess until she gets to finish the job. That's because boxers get a great sense of accomplishment and empowerment from marking something off as "done," i.e., digging the biggest, widest and deepest hole on Earth. We finish what we start.

Humans need to learn that an "almost done" takes up valuable mindshare. Working on tasks in fits and starts can also be a highly inefficient use of time, whether you are digging holes or sitting at the computer. For example, time-management gurus tell people to block off specific times of the day to read and respond to e-mail—an hour in the morning and an hour in the afternoon is common advice. The problem is that most people don't take enough time to read and respond carefully. They skim through the first few sentences of an e-mail and send a hasty, piece-meal response that requires even more back-and-forth. Now they are wasting the time of two people!

It's much better to prepare yourself mentally and physically to finish what you start. Clear your desk, organize your papers, shut the door and drop your furry friend off at dog day care for a few hours of supervised fun. Break tasks down into pieces and get to work. And if there are tasks that you never seem to finish (or that stand in the way of finishing more important things), then outsource them. Case in point: My two-legged mom is a neatnik with the superhuman ability to see every single dog hair in the office and house. She finally realized that her time was better spent with clients, not with picking dog hair out of the photocopy machine, and hired a cleaning service.

One last comment: If there is something that you really, truly can't seem to finish, then maybe it wasn't meant to be. Take it off your action plan and get rid of the guilt that goes along with it.

RUN WITH THE BALL

We all have our quirks; they are what make us unique. Me, I don't drink water that's been standing still. The irony is that I live in one of the dog-friendliest cities in the country, where every business has a water-filled dog bowl on its doorstep, but I'm fussy when it comes to matters of hydration. For example, I won't go jogging with my humans unless one of them caddies a bottle of water and pours it for me. I prefer water that moves, especially water that shoots straight out of a garden hose. It doesn't matter that I catch only a few drops at a time or that it's very uncomfortable when it gets up my nose.

What's my point? Well, the human ritual of "information gathering" is a lot like drinking from a garden hose— you catch only a few bits of information at a time, but you still feel like you are drowning. Worse, you can lose focus and get distracted from the true task at hand. Besides, it's impossible to collect every single piece of relevant information. Humans procrastinate by saying they need all the details. Well, you'll never have all the details. Too much data can even make you forget what you were looking for in the first place.

For better or worse, technology delivers information faster than the time it takes a hungry boxer to devour an entire cheese pizza. Yet there is a fine line between information *down*load and information *over*load. Unlike humans, dogs don't get caught in analysis paralysis. When we face choices and opportunities, we trust our instincts and we go for it—better to goof than to not goof at all!

Dogs get the information we need to make a decision and we make the decision, because good enough can be good enough—and because there's something to be said for good old-fashioned mystery and surprise. Dogs don't research and plan all the little details of life. We don't need a GPS to find the nearest dog park, and we don't Google the names of our friends to determine who'll make a worthy play pal. We'd rather be surprised by what life brings our way, because it makes the prospect of every brand new day just that much more exciting.

Another smart dog trait is that once we've made a decision, we don't look back. We keep our eyes on the prize. When I run after my ball—when it's not stuck under the couch, that is—I concentrate all my energy and attention on where I want to go. I focus on the path that is ahead of me and I don't look sideways or over my shoulder. Why? Because I know that it is bad luck to look where you don't want to go. My two-legged dad learned this lesson the hard way. While mountain biking in the Arizona desert, he focused on trying to avoid the sharp and spiny cacti that were growing alongside the bike trail, but managed to veer off the path and drive straight into a saguaro. The fancy explanation for Dad's bicycle crash is "target fixation," but the lesson itself is fairly simple: Obsessing over things you want to avoid can make you crash straight into them. Instead, look straight ahead, stay positive and always focus on success.

BELLA'S SOUND BITES

- Get enough sleep—without it, you'll be unfocused, unproductive and unhealthy.

- Don't buy into the myth of multitasking. It is impossible to do many things at once and do any of them well.

- Sharpen your focus and manage your time by planning your day, dumping the distractions and finishing what you've started.

- Run with the ball. When an opportunity comes along, gather enough information to make a decision and make a decision.

....

Chapter 5

Communication:
Sit, Stay and Listen

A good listener is not only popular everywhere,
but after a while he gets to know something.

– *Wilson Mizner*

No one appreciates the very special genius of your
conversation as the dog does.

– *Christopher Morley*

A degree from puppy kindergarten is the canine equivalent of a certificate from charm school, where humans learn to behave properly and get invited to do fun things. I know, because since I earned my certificate, I've been invited to my fair share of business meetings, networking events, picnics and parties, and I've learned to mooch with style. Catered events are the best, since hors d'oeuvres always seem to find their way from clumsy human fingers to the floor. I am now quite mannerly about foraging for crumbs around people's feet.

Of course, people don't realize that while I'm scrounging for food, I'm also eavesdropping on their conversations. My conclusion: Humans talk way too much and listen way too little.

The problem is that humans are easily distracted. They cut each other off and hijack each other's sentences. When they're not talking about themselves, you can tell they're busy trying to come up with the next thing to say about themselves. It's no surprise that many people admit that they are more likely to confide in their pets than their spouses, significant others, family members or friends. The reason is that a pet will sit down, look you in the eye and show interest and enthusiasm as if his or her next meal depended on it (which it does, but that's a topic for another discussion).

HEAR VS. LISTEN

I may have floppy ears, but I still hear five times better than most humans. For example, I can hear the rustle of a cheese wrapper from a mile away. I suspect that's the reason my two-legged mom used to get so frustrated with me at the off-leash dog park. She knows that I can hear her—even when I pretend I can't. It used to be when she barked the command "Bella, come," for instance, I'd grab my red rubber ball and run in the other direction. Why? I knew she was getting ready to leash me up and take me home. That's why she enrolled me in a second semester of obedience school. I'm better now. Usually.

Ears are designed for both hearing and listening, but there's a big difference between the two. When sound waves hit the ear and get processed by the brain, that's hearing. Hearing doesn't require any extra effort, which means you can hear something even when you don't want to hear it, especially if you're not too excited about it. This would be commands such as "Bella, come," or "Bella, drop that piece of ham right now."

Listening, on the other hand, involves paying attention not only to what someone says but also to how they say it, and responding appropriately. Good listeners may not always agree with what's being said, but they learn faster, make friends easier and avoid misunderstandings—all of which are valuable skills to have whether you go through life on two legs or four.

So what's the secret to becoming a better listener? Learning to wag your tail more than your tongue:

- Give the person who is speaking your full and undivided attention. Dogs don't always like to make direct eye contact, but it's the polite thing for humans to do when they are speaking with other humans. Stand straight and don't fidget. Keep your head up, your eyes forward and your paws planted firmly on the ground. Even if a tray of mouthwatering bacon-wrapped hot dogs passes by—stay focused!

- Pay attention to the speaker's body language to understand what's not being said. Like a dog who wags her tail in wide, friendly sweeps, a speaker who is animated and smiling is eager to share. A speaker with his arms folded across his chest, on the other hand, may not appreciate being hounded for additional information.

- Don't think about answers, actions or arguments while someone is still speaking. You can't respond appropriately if you don't listen carefully. For example, I heard, "Bella, come," and hightailed it straight out of the dog park. My two-legged mom insists that she said, "Bella, come get a cookie and then you can go back and play." Thanks to this unfortunate misunderstanding, I didn't get the cookie. I also spent the next eight Saturday mornings back in obedience school.

- Show that you are interested. I like to look up at the person doing the talking and tilt my head 45 degrees to acknowledge his or her brilliance. Since this may lead to neck cramps in humans, I suggest a slight nod or an occasional "Hmm," "Woof," "And?" or "Then?" to show that you're awake and engaged.

- Finally, remember that the letters in the word "listen" can be rearranged to spell the word "silent." Most humans just want to be listened to, which is easy, because listening doesn't mean you need to have all the answers or fix a problem. You know why people are comforted by talking to their dogs? Because we just listen; we don't make judgments or offer unsolicited advice. An "uncomfortable silence" doesn't exist in the canine world, which explains why dogs happily spend hours sitting at your feet without making a single sound.

The bottom line? Dogs and humans have two ears and one mouth and should use them in that proportion.

CHEW YOUR WORDS CAREFULLY

As a breed, boxers are relatively quiet. We're not as silent as the "barkless" basenji, but neither are we the yip-yappy dog who drives the whole neighborhood up a tree. We know that the best way to get people to sit up and pay attention is to use our voices thoughtfully. That's why, on the rare occasion when I do bark or growl, my officemates sit up and take notice.

Unfortunately, too many humans flap their gums without giving thought to what they are saying or how they sound. Reality television hasn't helped. All you have to do is watch a few hours to get the idea that it's OK to share every single thing that pops into your head (sadly, even the talented, handsome boxer who won *Greatest American Dog* couldn't save the show from its mindless blather). The tell-all trend makes for very juicy network ratings, but it hasn't done a thing to teach humans how to communicate in a way that conveys confidence or generates personal or professional respect.

Now that I have all four paws up on my soapbox, let me address another problem: "filler"—and I'm not referring to the nasty stuff that's added to cheap pet food (although both types of filler can cause serious gastric distress). I'm talking about the words and phrases that humans are so fond of and that have no nutritional value, such as "uh huh," "um," "like," "actually," "totally," "I mean" and "you know." The same goes for wishy-washy language, like "I was thinking that we might like to go to the dog park today." What's wrong with something direct and to the point, like "Let's go to the dog park"? If you can't communicate your ideas surely and clearly, how will you sell them to others?

Dogs understand that the most effective way to make a point is to say less, not more. Dog trainers know this, too, which is why they give a command only once. For example, if you want your dog Peanut to sit, you say, "Peanut, sit." Yet visit any training class and you'll find a pack of confused dogs and frustrated people shouting, "Peanut, can you sit? Sit down, Peanut. Peanut, sit. OK, now sit. Good boy, sit. Please sit. S-I-T!" Not surprisingly, Peanut has tuned out and is chewing on the end of his leash.

It's also important to understand that if you are always whining, wheedling, nagging or cajoling, you are unwittingly training people to ignore you. Plus, nobody likes to be nagged or yelled at. It doesn't matter if you are a human, a dog—or a whale.

Case Study:
Lessons from Shamu

While doing research for a book on exotic animal trainers, journalist Amy Sutherland realized that many of the trainers' techniques could work on the human animals in her own life—especially her husband. Sutherland's article "What Shamu Taught Me About a Happy Marriage" was the most e-mailed article of *The New York Times* online in 2006 and became the basis of her popular book *What Shamu Taught Me About Life, Love, and Marriage.*

Sutherland explains that progressive animal trainers think of training as two-way communication. Their goal isn't to teach animals to be obedient, but to be engaged, and they rely on positive rewards instead of punishment or force. They also know when to keep quiet. According to Sutherland, humans often sabotage themselves with their own language. They say one thing when they mean another, and then they try to clear things up with more words.

Animal trainers, however, know that words are precious—they must be precise and perfectly timed. From that Sutherland learned that hers was the only behavior she could control. So she stopped nagging her husband about leaving his dirty laundry on the floor and started offering praise for the many things he did well. Soon, he was picking up the laundry without being prompted. That dynamic led to more considerate, involved interaction between them without tension. By learning when to speak and when to hold her tongue, Sutherland made her marriage even stronger.

....

The lessons in Sutherland's book apply to every relationship, whether it's with your spouse, your boss, your co-workers or your two-legged and four-legged friends. Be deliberate not only in what you say but also when, where and how you say it.

COMMUNICATE WITH CONFIDENCE

In puppy kindergarten, I had a huge crush on a black and tan German shepherd puppy named Baxter. I even doodled "Bella Hearts Baxter" in the margins of my training manual. Needless to say, I was disappointed when he dropped out of class about halfway through the semester. According to the gossip mill, his two-legged humans thought that puppy kindergarten was a waste of time and money, since Baxter never seemed to listen to them.

I never got to know Baxter very well, but I'm pretty sure that he knew exactly what his humans were asking him to do when they hollered "sit" and "stay" from across the classroom. It's just that he chose not to, but it was easy to see why. Baxter's humans were fussy and fidgety. They didn't have to speak a single word to make it clear they were anxious and out of control. They were the ones who needed training, not Baxter. Dogs look up to humans who are calm, relaxed and confident. Even when you think we aren't looking, we're watching your movements and learning from your actions and reactions. It's why I like hanging out with my friend Doug Duncan. Doug is a certified dog trainer and owner of Doggy Business Dog Training & Lodging in Portland, Ore. When my humans go out of town for a few days, I get to ride around town with Doug in his big red truck and observe how he trains his fellow humans. The humans think he's training their dogs, but it's really the other way around. Clever, huh?

Doug reminds people how important it is to stay calm and patient and to use clear signals when working with their dogs. Because dogs are visual learners, Doug leads training exercises where the two-legged students are allowed to communicate with their dogs only through hand signals and other nonverbal clues, because too much background "noise" gets in the way and makes it harder to concentrate. It's the same reason we pay better attention to people who speak softly because they are self-confident than to those who bark loudly because they are not. To be a leader you have to communicate like one—not just with words, but also with a calm, positive demeanor that projects inner confidence and credibility.

Oh, one last bit of advice about nonverbal communication: Heed your mother's advice and stand up straight! A confident dog has his head up, his ears pricked and all four feet planted squarely on the ground. Likewise, humans who pull their shoulders back, push their chests up and out, and sit up straight have more confidence than people who slouch. Don't tell people you're in charge—show them you are.

SELF-PROMOTION,
OR WHEN IT'S OK TO BE A HOT DOG

Dogs don't question their own instincts. If we believe in something, we go for it; we don't need to drum up interest or support with what people call dog-and-pony shows (honestly, the terms they use!). And even though I believe in the "less is more" philosophy, I also know that the times they are a-changin'. Sometimes, you just have to put yourself out there and strut your stuff!

Why? Because a degree from puppy kindergarten, even if it's Ivy League, is not enough to get you noticed anymore. As big companies slash jobs and all the "traditional" places of employment start to disappear, it doesn't do you any good to be the strong and silent type. In the modern working world, you have to be your own best marketing machine. Nobody can, or will, promote you as well as you promote yourself (unless you are a Beverly Hills Chihuahua, with enough pocket change to hire your own agent).

Please don't misunderstand. I'm not talking about strutting around town and bragging about being the biggest or fastest dog at the dog park. That's just putting on the dog (or human, as the case may be). Instead of talking about your own accomplishments, self-promotion is about letting people know that you love what you do and that you do it better than anyone else. It's about sharing your ideas so others can learn from you and be inspired to take action. For instance, animal behaviorist and veterinarian Dr. Ian Dunbar didn't invent positive reinforcement training, but he was the first to popularize it for most people. His books, videos and training sessions have helped millions of humans turn away from dominance training and communicate with their dogs in a fun and positive way. Dr. Dunbar's dog-friendly methods have influenced many dog trainers—and, through them, people who live with dogs.

The bottom line? You can't share your message or your ideas with the world if people don't know who you are or if they take you for granted. People like to be around other talented, confident people because those are the people most likely to recognize and appreciate talent in others. So don't be afraid to engage in self-promotion when it's well deserved and appropriate. Just make sure that you have something to say and that you say it well. And follow Franklin D. Roosevelt's advice and "be sincere; be brief; be seated."

WHEN TO HOLD YOUR TONGUE

Last, but not least, the best way to communicate your own success is never to speak negatively about someone else's. Badmouthing and gossip are not only bad energy but also a doggone waste of words. Instead, focus on your own achievements and learn to communicate surely and clearly while projecting a confident, positive attitude. After all, like attracts like.

BELLA'S SOUND BITES

- Become a better listener by wagging your tail more than your tongue.

- Choose your words carefully. Be deliberate in not only *what* you say, but also *when, where* and *how* you say it.

- Communicate like a leader, not just with words but also with a calm, positive demeanor that projects confidence and credibility.

- Broadcast your own success by never speaking negatively about someone else's.

Chapter 6

Persistence:
Never Let Go
of the Rope

Be like a postage stamp. Stick to it until you get there.

– Harvey Mackay

Life is like a dogsled team. If you ain't the lead dog,
the scenery never changes.

– Lewis Grizzard

Grit. Pluck. Tenacity. Persistence. Resilience. Whatever
you want to call it, we dogs have it. Fortunately for humans we are more than happy to teach you how to stay on
track and not let the bumps in the road discourage you.
For example, one of my all-time favorite activities is tug-
of-war, and my favorite sparring partner is my two-legged
dad. However, I usually have to bait him into playing with

me. My strategy is to sneak under his desk and wait until he's fully absorbed in his work, or on the phone with an important client (they're all important, he says, and he's right), and then start jamming his leg with a rope toy.

His response is predictable. First, he'll say, "I'm busy right now" and then, "Go bug somebody else." But I know that he has to hang up the phone sometime and if I continue to jam the rope into his leg, he'll eventually give in. Once the game starts, I don't let go for anyone or anything—not even when Dad gives the "drop it" command in his most authoritative voice. (Of course, I realize this admission opens me up to analysis and criticism by dog trainers everywhere, including my own, to which I say, "All's fair in love and tug-of-war." Besides, I'll totally drop the rope toy for Mom. I know who's really in charge.)

EMBRACE THE WORD "NO"

Whether I'm crushing the rope toy into Dad's leg, or dive-bombing the kitchen every time I hear the refrigerator door open, I am fully prepared to hear 10 "no's" for every "yes." Do I get discouraged? No. Do I take it personally? Absolutely not. The word "no" doesn't hurt my feelings, crush my self-confidence or prevent me from trying again.

Fortunately, the word "no" doesn't discourage my mom, either. In fact, it only strengthens her resolve. I guess this explains her four-year campaign to convince my dad, who never had any fuzzy four-legged companions as a child, that getting a dog—a boxer named Bella, to be precise—

would be the best thing to ever happen to him (next to her, of course). Everywhere they went, if Mom spotted a dog walking nearby, she'd drag Dad over for a friendly tête-à-tête. His resistance was strong, but her persistence was stronger. This turned out to be a very good thing for all of us, of course.

Dogs and boxer-crazy humans aren't the only ones who are persistent, however. Cats also know how to dig in their claws and hang on tight. In fact, a few have even clawed themselves into my circle of friends, including a calico named Courage.

Case Study:
Courage the Cat and "Go for No!"

You would think that a cat named Courage would have no fear, but you'd be wrong. Courage was turned in to a shelter by a family that was moving and couldn't take him along. Being in a strange place was almost more than he could bear, and he stayed in the back of his cage away from all the noise and commotion. Finally, a man came over, and though Courage was afraid, he let the man rub his head. Before he knew it, Courage was on his way home to live with his new humans, Richard Fenton and Andrea Waltz.

Courage didn't know it at the time, but Richard and Andrea had written a book called *Go for No!* and created a sales program around "failing your way to success." These days, Courage likes to think he has taught Richard and Andrea everything they know about being fearless. They're OK with that because Courage has, in fact, taught them a lot about the power of persistence.

Like most cats, Courage doesn't let the word "no" faze him. For example, Courage knows that he'll hear a lot of "no's" when he starts clawing the dining room chairs, which are far more interesting to him than his scratching posts. And even though Courage has an extensive list of fears—the vacuum, ceiling fan, balloons, loud noises—the word "no" is not among them. Why? His humans have taught him that he can achieve anything if he is willing to hear those two letters often enough.

For Courage, "no" is just one step on the path to success. He always pushes just a bit further to see how much he can accomplish. For instance, Courage knows he's not allowed on the kitchen counter; getting caught always elicits a loud "no!" shouted from across the room. But when there's a big, worthy goal like fresh shrimp on the countertop, Courage doesn't dream of letting something as small and inconsequential as the word "no" stop him. He knows that with big risks come big rewards, and that "no" doesn't mean "never"—it just means "not yet."

www.goforno.com

Courage would say that the only way to get a mouthful of fresh shrimp is to "go for no!" Unfortunately, too many humans are afraid to go after their dreams because they let the word "no" stop them in their tracks. They get discouraged, lose momentum and stop trying to reach their goals.

The problem is that they have the wrong ideas about success and failure. They see themselves in the middle, with success (yes) on one end and failure (no) on the other. But most everyone has to experience failure to achieve success. Everything you want to achieve is waiting on the other side of "no," as long as you are willing to keep hearing it. What's more, if you're not hearing "no" often enough, you're not on to something big. If you give up too soon, you won't succeed.

SHAKE OFF SETBACKS

My favorite dog park is next to a playground. Summer or winter, rain or shine, there are always gaggles of kids playing on the swings and riding the small bouncy ponies. (What do you call a group of kids anyway? A gaggle? A flock? A herd?) The amazing thing about these miniature two-leggeds is that when they fall, most of them dust themselves off and get right back into the saddle again without even whimpering. The only people who freak out are their parents.

Why is that? Because unlike dogs, humans grow into adulthood and become afraid to try. They lose their instinct for taking risks and shaking off setbacks. This is a shame, since determination can be more important than talent in achieving long-term goals. In fact, researchers say it takes 10,000 hours of practice to become an expert in your field. Wow! That means you'll make many mistakes and hear a lot of "no's" before achieving what many people like to call "an overnight success."

Setbacks don't have to stop you, but the way that you deal with them can. For inspiration, consider these seven humans (and one dog) who got up, shook off criticism and defeat and went on to achieve great success:

- J.K. Rowling: 12 publishers rejected her book about a boy wizard named Harry Potter.
- Walt Disney: A newspaper editor fired him saying "he lacked imagination and had no good ideas."
- Charles Schulz: The high school yearbook staff rejected his *Peanuts* cartoons.
- Lucille Ball: She was dismissed from drama school and told to "try any other profession."
- Vincent van Gogh: He completed more than 800 paintings, yet sold only one during his lifetime.
- Michael Jordan: He was cut from his high school basketball team.
- Thomas Edison: A teacher said that he was "too stupid" to learn anything.
- Moose the dog: His first family gave him up because he was "too hard to handle": He chased cats, couldn't be housebroken, chewed everything in sight and liked to escape. This underappreciated Jack Russell terrier went on to earn $10,000 per episode for playing Eddie on the hit TV show *Frasier*. (By the way, if any Hollywood casting agents are reading this book, I'm reviewing scripts.)

Dogs aren't perfect. We take risks and we make mistakes, but we shake off setbacks and take off running again. In a world of instant gratification, it's easy to forget that anything worth doing is inherently challenging. Obstacles can make you more determined to succeed and give you a good story to tell when you are a big success.

Case Study:
Greenies
....

Ivan the Samoyed lived with Joe and Judy Roetheli in Kansas City, Mo. Ivan was a loyal member of the family, but he had horrible breath—so bad that Judy asked her husband, Dr. Joe Roetheli, to do something about it. He tinkered in the kitchen and came up with the formula for Greenies, a digestible dental chew in the shape of a green toothbrush. Joe quit his steady job as an agricultural economist, and he and Judy threw themselves into the business full time.

For three years, the Roethelis had virtually no income. They racked up $200,000 in credit card debt and talked family and friends into investing in the business to keep afloat. They went to dozens of banks to ask for a loan and got rejected every single time— talk about "going for no!" Fortunately, the Roethelis were like their dog Ivan (and every other dog in the world). They didn't take the rejection personally. They didn't hold grudges when people said their idea was crazy. They simply refused to give up. They held on to their dream like it was a rope toy in the ultimate game of tug-of-war.

What started as a homemade breath-freshening treat eventually expanded to a packaged product carried in all 50 states and exported to more than 60 countries. When the Roethelis sold the company to Mars Inc. in 2006, they had shipped more than 750 million Greenies and theirs was the eighth-largest pet food/treat company in the world. Today, Joe is the CEO of eight different entrepreneurial ventures. He and Judy launched the Roetheli Lil' Red Foundation (*www.lilredfoundation.com*), a nonprofit that builds villages in the impoverished country of Guyana. Here, too, the Roetheli persistence has paid off, since dealing with Third World bureaucracy is not for the faint of heart (the word "no" being all too common worldwide).

....

BE YOUR OWN DOG

I'm a goofball, and thanks to the Internet anyone who types the keywords "Bella the Boxer" and "home alone" in most search engines can see that I'm not exaggerating. That's because my oh-so-clever humans thought it'd be great fun to set up a hidden "Bella cam" to watch what I do when I'm left alone for an hour or two. Lucky for me, the camera timed out before it could catch me shredding the bed pillows and adorning myself with goose feathers.

Am I embarrassed because thousands of strangers have watched the video and know that I suffer from bouts of boredom when left alone? Not at all. Dogs aren't afraid of what others think. We don't care if the rest of the world sees us looking silly or making mistakes. We know that if we don't put ourselves out into the world, we won't get as many cookies or belly rubs in return.

What if Charles Shulz had given up after the editors of his high school yearbook rejected his *Peanuts* cartoons? There would be no quirky little dog named Snoopy who lounges on his doghouse and whose best friend is a strange yellow bird named Woodstock.

What if Carol Gardner had listened to people who said you have to be human and thin, rich, young or wrinkle-free to be successful? Nobody would know about Zelda, the full-figured English bulldog with a serious underbite who makes people smile with her sassy sayings.

Dogs follow their own instincts. We don't worry about being judged or criticized by others because, quite frankly, life is much too short—especially in dog years—to be anyone else but ourselves. We're also not so self-absorbed that we think all eyes are on us, the exception being the poofy show dogs at the Westminster Kennel Club Dog Show. Most people have too much going on in their own lives to have the time to judge others. You can't please all people all the time, so there is no point in trying. There are people who love boxers and there are people who (gasp) don't. There's nothing I can do about that, except to be the best boxer I can be.

Be your own dog and don't let what other people think keep you from taking risks and pursuing your dreams. Really, there is no other way to be.

PERSISTENT OR JUST STUBBORN?

I'll admit it: Boxers are headstrong and don't give up easily. Sometimes, that's a good thing. For example, it took me three full weeks of nonstop head-banging to learn how to let myself in and out of the house via the dog door. To a human, a dog door is nothing more than a swinging plastic flap. To a dog, the door is freedom. It means going outside whenever you want to, without having to ask for permission. It means running back inside when it starts to rain or when there are the faintest of footsteps in the kitchen (which means a snack is possible). A dog door opens up a whole new world of opportunity—which is what makes it so scary.

At first, the door frightened me. I worried about what might be lurking on the other side. And that I wouldn't be able to get back inside. Still, I knew I had to push through to the other side. Every day I took one step farther. I started by boxing the door with my paws. Then I pressed my nose up against the plastic flap. Next, I stuck one paw through, followed by two paws and soon thereafter, all four legs. Once I launched myself into the great outdoors (i.e., the fenced-in backyard), I never looked back.

Today, I don't give the dog door a second thought. My humans complain that the constant *slap-slap-slap* of the door swinging back and forth on its hinges makes it sound like we live in a Western saloon. Despite their protests, I know they're proud of me for persisting and not giving up.

Stubbornness, on the other hand, is doing the same thing over and over again and expecting something different to happen each time. It rarely pays off, a lesson that my two-legged mom learned in what I like to call the "dog class incident." She had enrolled us in a class with the most talked-about dog trainer in town to help improve my manners. (What can I say? We boxers have an exuberant zest for life, and we love to jump on people and give them big hugs and sloppy kisses, which is apparently not something many humans appreciate.)

In any case, this trainer was the "buzz" of the dog park, and it took some jockeying to get a spot in her class, but my two-legged mom persevered and the trainer finally accepted us as her students. From the beginning of the first session, however, I knew it was a terrible fit. The trainer was moody and militant, and when she said, "zig," I automatically went "zag."

It was clearly not a productive relationship. Yet Mom dug in her heels and insisted that we press on, even though the trainer caused her an inordinate amount of stress plus a couple hundred bucks. It wasn't until week four that Mom finally agreed with me that she was stubborn and should stop attending class just to complete it. When the trainer lost patience with us yet again, Mom told her "&#@!*" and we left (it's no secret that Mom is the real watchdog in our family). Eventually, we found a new teacher who understands and appreciates boxers and their high energy and enthusiasm. With the right coaching, I'm getting better at keeping all four feet on the floor.

The point is that a stubborn dog refuses to change. However, a persistent dog believes that she has what it takes to make something happen and finds alternative ways to do it. Persistence also means admitting that one method, or trainer, does not fit all. When something isn't working, you find a way to get around it—and then get around it. It's the only way to become top dog.

BELLA'S SOUND BITES

- Embrace the word "no." Rejection is just one step on the path to success.

- Shake off setbacks like a dog shakes off water. If you don't fail, you don't learn.

- Follow your own instincts. Other people's opinions shouldn't keep you from taking risks and pursuing your dreams.

- Be persistent, not stubborn. Top dogs admit when something's not working and find a way around it.

Chapter 7

Camaraderie:
Build Your Pack

There are two kinds of people—those who come into a
room and say, "Well, here I am!" and those who come in
and say, "Ah, there you are."

– Frederick L. Collins

When a man's best friend is his dog,
that dog has a problem.

– Edward Abbey

Dogs instinctively know how to connect with their fellow
dogs. Every four-legged fur ball I've ever met likes to get
out, sniff around, greet old friends and make new ones.
We know the value of building a pack.

However, humans like to say that it's "every man for
himself," which is just silly. Take it from a dog: It takes a
pack of colleagues, coaches, mentors and friends to make
a successful life.

My own pack is made up of hundreds of dogs and humans. I've met many of them around town at business conferences, art fairs, dog parks, the veterinarian's office, the pet supply store and the corner café.

My network also includes people and pets I've met online. An artist in Seattle used a photo from my website to paint an oil portrait that was featured in a local art gallery and then appeared in a calendar sold in catalogs and bookstores across America. A boxer lover in Texas created some of my graphic design materials. A four-legged suitor from West Virginia who reads my blog sent me a Valentine's bouquet made of colorful felt flowers (one of which I promptly swallowed; it miraculously reappeared a few days later—so much for Valentine's Day romance).

Indeed, I love meeting new people and making new friends so much that it makes me sad to know there are humans who isolate themselves in their work and their jobs. For those who work at home or are stuck in a cubicle all day long, it's an easy trap to fall into. But humans, like dogs, are pack animals who aren't meant to go through life alone.

So why are so many humans lonelier than they were just 10 years ago? Why are there people who have dozens or even hundreds of Facebook friends and Twitter followers yet nobody besides their pets to confide in?

THE DIGITAL BUBBLE

Technology can be pretty cool. Thanks to the Internet, I don't ever have to leave my house to meet other dogs and their people, something I appreciate on a cold, rainy winter day when I don't feel like getting my paws wet and muddy at the dog park. The Internet may even rival the long-handled plastic ball launcher for coolness. (Anyone who lives with a dog like me who is obsessed with chasing slobbery tennis balls for hours on end knows what a great toy this is!)

On the other hand, a ball launcher has one gigantic advantage over the Internet: It forces humans to step away from their desks and head out with their dogs to the nearest park, beach or backyard. This is a very good thing, because the strongest personal and professional relationships are those that develop *away* from the computer.

I'm sure that some people would disagree with me. After all, the Internet makes it easier for people to connect with people they already know or who are just like them. Unfortunately, it also makes them less likely to seek out people with diverse backgrounds or opinions. For proof, go to a café or coffee shop and watch how many humans are typing, texting or tweeting their online friends instead of striking up a conversation with the people sitting right next to them. Chances are, little kids and dogs are the only ones running around having any real-world interactions.

Let me give you a more personal example. Online, I like to spend most of my time chatting with other boxers and their boxer-loving humans. I guess it has something to do with "boxers of a feather flock together." In real life, however, I don't meet nearly as many boxers as I would like. For example, on a recent weeklong vacation at the beach with my humans, there wasn't a single boxer in sight. Not that I cared; I played with the other dogs and learned how to sniff out razor clams from a Havanese named Harry. Thanks to Harry, I learned a new skill and made a brand new friend whose breed I hadn't heard of until then. Neither of these things would have happened if I hadn't bounded out from behind the computer screen.

SOCIALIZATION: IT'S NOT JUST FOR DOGS

When I was just a few months old, my humans enrolled me in puppy kindergarten. What a circus it was! Every week, I experienced a brand new and slightly crazy situation. There were other puppies, vacuum cleaners, wheelchairs, shopping carts, men with beards, odd sounds and sudden, loud noises. Fortunately, there were no clowns— and I say "fortunately" because I can vouch for the fact that being afraid of clowns is something many humans and dogs share.

The point is that puppy kindergarten introduces young and impressionable dogs to new people and experiences so they aren't afraid of them later in life. In the canine world, the process is called socialization, and it is the key to raising a happy, friendly, predictable dog who plays well with others. The more you isolate your dog, the more likely he or she is to lack confidence and be shy, anxious or even aggressive.

Socialization doesn't stop when a puppy grows up, either. I go to dog day care for a few hours every week to meet new dogs and to practice sharing my toys ("practice" being what my mom calls the "operative" word). Some weekends I drop by an organized "dog social" for the chance to romp with an alternative pack of pups and to learn from a different team of trainers.

Sure, a dog's confidence comes from exposure to a variety of people, places and situations, especially a working dog's confidence. The same is true for humans. Thankfully, it's never too late for you to open yourself up to new people and new experiences. To succeed in life, you need to play well with others and make real-life connections. To do that you have to get out of your cubby, cubicle—or cell, as the case may be.

Case Study:
Puppies and Prisoners
....

Since 1997, an organization called Puppies Behind Bars (PBB) has relied on prison inmates to raise service dogs to work with the disabled or in law enforcement. Specially bred, these dogs spend the first 18 months of their lives with the inmates, who teach them basic obedience and good manners to socialize them.

Founded by Gloria Gilbert Stoga, PBB began with five puppies in the Bedford Hills Correctional Facility, New York State's only maximum-security prison for women. Today, the program operates in six different prisons and has graduated hundreds of service dogs and explosive-detection canines. In 2006, PBB created the Dog Tags program through which it donates fully trained service dogs to wounded soldiers coming home from Iraq and Afghanistan.

The program is successful because both puppies and inmates learn to become confident and contributing members of society. Since prisons are like their own small cities, puppies are exposed to a variety of different situations every day, accompanying their companions to their jobs and tagging along to prison libraries, laundries, chapels and dining rooms. During the day, dogs and humans attend training classes together. At night, they share a cell for more one-on-one bonding. Inmates are responsible for every aspect of puppy care and training, and the requirements for their jobs are rigorous.

Inevitably, the puppies must leave the prison. Some continue their formal training as working dogs, and others serve as companion animals.

For many of the inmates, raising a puppy is the first real responsibility they have ever had. Along the way, they learn patience, teamwork and discipline. They learn how to explain their job to other inmates and prison staff, and how to act as ambassadors for the program. They learn how to give and receive unconditional love. In a nutshell, they learn to look outside themselves and become socialized to the world around them. *www.puppiesbehindbars.com*

MAKE FRIENDS LIKE A DOG

One of my favorite outings is an afternoon stroll to the local bakery. While my humans satisfy their craving for caffeine, I sit outside and look adorable (to be honest, it's not hard—I'm a boxer). I get lots of attention, and the more people I interact with, the more energized I become. Of course, some of this energy comes from sugar. Can I help it if people holding delicious muffins and pastries bend down to my level?

Imagine my shock, then, to find out that very few humans share my canine enthusiasm for getting out and meeting new people. Only a fraction—10–20 percent, according to some surveys—actually like to network nose-to-nose, or, rather, face-to-face. The rest avoid it or hate it altogether. But even the smartest and most self-reliant human being won't get very far in life without his or her own pack of supporters.

I think that part of the problem is that humans stumble over their own language. They talk about "networking" as a specific event where they're expected to dole out business cards and ask for something in return, such as an appointment, a sale, a referral or a job interview. That would be like me showing up at a new dog day care facility, doing a cursory sniff-around and then asking the other dogs to give up their tennis balls. Even if I did have my own fancy business cards to hand out, it would be awkward and unproductive.

The better way—the dogpreneur way—to build a network is to think in terms of "connecting." Whereas "networking" is an activity with a beginning and an end, "connecting" is a way of life. Dogs make friends to make friends, not to drum up business or push their own agenda. Motivational speaker and author Zig Ziglar said it best: "You can have everything in life you want if you will just help enough other people get what they want."

As soon as humans stop thinking about what they can get out of a relationship and start thinking about what they can offer someone else, everything becomes a networking opportunity. Whether it's called karma, the Golden Rule, giver's gain or plain old dog sense, good things automatically happen when you concentrate on being useful to others.

REACH OUT AND PAW SOMEONE

Fortunately, you don't have to love the spotlight to make connections. If you want to network better than anyone else, you just need to think like a dog.

Make Others Feel Good

As soon as my humans walk through the front door, I give them a series of big, sloppy kisses. It doesn't matter if they've been gone for a minute or an hour; I do it because it makes us all happy. If you're nervous about walking into a room full of strangers, try giving people a friendly smile and a warm "hello." You'll put everyone at ease, including yourself.

Volunteer To Be Lead Dog

I know a Welsh corgi who thinks it's his job to herd people around the neighborhood by nipping at their heels. This isn't my idea of a working dog. Instead, I suggest volunteering for a designated job like greeting people at the front door or handing out name tags. It will boost your confidence and give you a chance to meet people before they gravitate toward their friends or make a beeline for the buffet. You'll find that most people will be glad when you approach them, since they, too, are looking for someone to talk with.

Sniff Out a Connection

Humans waste way too much time chitchatting about the weather. Seriously, you know what I'm saying. Networking is about making meaningful connections, so ask thoughtful questions. If possible, do your homework and learn something about the person you are meeting. And, if you're really stuck for words, talk about your dog, your goldfish, or, if the situation is truly dire, your neighbor's cat (because you wouldn't have one of those creatures yourself, would you?). You'll be amazed at how many people have pets and love to talk about them, and how easy it is to transition to other topics once you've made a genuine connection.

Don't Come On Too Strong

I was enjoying myself at a dog social when a hyperactive bull terrier pup charged straight at me. No, "Hello, my name is Spike," or "It's nice to meet you." Instead, he launched directly into inappropriate wrestling, and I'm embarrassed to admit that I growled at him. The lesson is to adjust your energy level to the other person's so that no meeting ever ends in a growl. When I meet someone for the first time, I'm careful (OK, pretty careful) not to over-whelm them if I sense they may not appreciate the typi-cal two-paws-off-the-ground boxer greeting. But if that same person gets down on his or her knees and opens their arms, I'm thrilled to oblige with a full-body tackle.

Stand Out From the Crowd

My two-legged dad wears a custom-designed name tag to events instead of a boring generic name tag. As for me, I wear collars with bright, boldly colored patterns that are hard to miss in a crowd. In the winter, I strut around town in a candy-apple-red fleece jacket that keeps me warm, gets tongues wagging and sparks some interesting conver-sations. If it's hard for you to introduce yourself to strang-ers, make it easier for them to approach you by standing out from everyone else. Putting your own spin on things makes people want to come to you.

Perk Up Your Ears

In the dog world, names are irrelevant. Rover, Fido, Spot—it doesn't matter. A quick sniff gives us all the personal information we need. Unfortunately, in the human world sniffing is considered weird and impolite. Dale Carnegie said that the sweetest sound in the world is the sound of a person's own name, which explains why many humans worry less about meeting others than simply forgetting their names. So, whether your ears point like a Dober-man pinscher's or flop like a basset hound's, perk them up and listen carefully when people introduce themselves. Shake paws to make a connection and take a few seconds to focus on that person. People appreciate it when you are interested in them and go out of your way to remember them by name.

Dig Out What's Different

I love driving out to the country with my humans for a chance to chat with the locals—the cows, the horses and the deer (but never, ever the skunks). They don't always appreciate my efforts, but I always try. The key to making friends like a dog is to always be curious. Never pass up an opportunity to meet someone new just because they don't walk, talk or look like you. Dogs know that mutually beneficial partnerships come in all shapes and sizes, and they have no problem looking past (or searching out) differences that most humans would think were too big to ignore.

Case Study:
Elephant Sanctuary

The nonprofit Elephant Sanctuary in Hohenwald, Tenn., operates on more than 2,700 acres of natural habitat and is a refuge for old, sick or needy African and Asian elephants who have been retired from zoos and circuses.

One of the residents is Tarra, an 8,700-pound Asian elephant who was captured from the wild in 1974 and who has been living at The Elephant Sanctuary since 1995. Like the other elephants at the sanctuary, Tarra has paired off with a buddy—except in Tarra's case, her best friend is not another pachyderm but a 35-pound mixed-breed dog with the fine name of Bella. Tarra and Bella are inseparable. They play, eat, drink, swim and sleep together. Bella trusts Tarra enough to lie under her friend's enormous elephant foot for a belly rub, and Tarra is fiercely protective of her canine companion.

In 2007, Bella was immobilized with a serious spinal cord injury that left her unable to move her legs or even wag her tail. For three weeks, she stayed inside the sanctuary office for observation and treatment— and every day for three weeks, Tarra stood outside the office's second-floor window and looked for her friend. The elephant showed such concern that the staff started carrying Bella out to see Tarra so they could spend some time together.

Fortunately, Bella recovered and was able to return to the sanctuary to roam with her pal. Since then, she and Tarra have become media sensations, reminding humans around the world that friendship comes in all sizes and that it's often the unlikeliest of pairings that are the strongest. *www.elephants.com*

....

TEAMWORK

In our office, Monday mornings are set aside for a weekly team meeting. The humans drink coffee and take notes while I supervise from a pillow in the middle of the room.

It's a great way to make sure that we all understand each other and that we are all working from the same page. Better yet, there are snacks. Dogs and humans make great teams outside the office, too. Together they go on dangerous search-and-rescue missions, move livestock across miles of farmland and haul themselves across the frozen tundra of Alaska for a chance to win the Iditarod. There's even something called canine freestyle, in which humans and dogs dance together to music (something I will never be able to experience firsthand thanks to my humans' complete lack of rhythm). Dogs and humans who are well-choreographed teams have learned to trust each other completely. A guide dog will refuse a command on purpose if he thinks it will lead to danger, like walking off a ledge or stepping into oncoming traffic. A handler must trust his dog enough to accept the dog's decision as the right one. There's no arguing or second-guessing in the middle of a crosswalk—the team makes its decision and moves on.

This is the kind of absolute trust that humans sometime have trouble building among themselves. Fortunately, animals have a way of helping humans break down any imaginary walls they may put up.

Case Study:
World Vets

Cathy King is a doctor of veterinary medicine and the CEO and founder of World Vets, a nonprofit that organizes veterinary missions in 24 developing countries around the world. The organization works with animal advocacy groups, the United States military, foreign governments and veterinary professionals abroad to provide aid for animals and to address public health issues.

World Vets sends its teams on one-week trips to places like Nicaragua, Honduras, Romania and Peru, where they work in clinics to do everything from trimming the hooves of working horses to spaying and neutering local cats and dogs. Surprisingly, every team includes at least two or three "lay assistants" who have no veterinary experience whatsoever. It's hard to imagine taking 18 strangers of varying ages and mixed experience and getting them to function like a well-oiled machine under challenging conditions. But World Vets does it over and over again, building lasting friendships that endure well beyond the trips.

How do they do it? By harnessing the power of teamwork. For example, Dr. King and her team leaders always rent a residence where everyone can stay together. They know that team members who live together are more likely to trust each other and be more comfortable asking questions in the field. And, rather than launch right into a stressful work situation, World Vets makes sure that every team spends one or two days first enjoying leisure activities together. That way, people have a chance to learn each other's strengths, weaknesses and quirks before working together in trying circumstances, like administering vaccinations to uncooperative farm animals in 90-degree heat.

When it comes to choosing team leaders, Dr. King looks for skilled veterinarians with upbeat personalities who don't insist on being in surgery all day long. Instead, team leaders must be willing to be "part camp counselor," seeing that every person gets out of the trip what he or she wants or needs while making sure the work gets done. Ultimately, the goal of World Vets is to build teams that are committed and accountable—to each other, to the animals whose lives are at stake and to the communities where people often wait long hours to get treatment for their beloved pets. *www.worldvets.org*

Luckily, you don't have to be a hero to be a great teammate. At the office, my job is to see that my two-legged co-workers get out from behind their computer screens every few hours. I make sure that they stay energized, enthusiastic and creative, and they make sure I get exercise, treats and belly rubs. We make an excellent team.

BELLA'S SOUND BITES

- Assemble your pack. The most successful people (and dogpreneurs) are those who surround themselves with a network of colleagues, coaches, mentors and friends.

- Step outside your digital bubble and make real-life connections; face-to-face socializing is what creates long-lasting, meaningful relationships.

- Make friends to make friends, not to push your own agenda. Good things happen when you find ways to make other people successful.

- Pull together as part of a team and you'll accomplish things you could never do on your own.

Chapter 8

Appreciation: Shake It Like You Mean It

The habit that has helped me the most is learning to be thankful. It is the greatest secret of success.

– Charlie Tremendous Jones

There is no psychiatrist in the world like a puppy licking your face.

– Ben Williams

Life is good!

To celebrate it, a couple of times a day I wind myself into a half-moon and wiggle my stub tail while dancing sideways across the floor like a crab. In boxer-speak, this is called "doing the kidney bean." It's a boxer's own silly way of showing both gratitude and appreciation for even the most basic things in life—shelter, food, water and belly rubs.

Humans tend to lump gratitude and appreciation together, but a dog will tell you that there is a difference. Think of it this way: Appreciation is gratitude in action. It's something you feel throughout your entire body, from the tip of your tongue to the end of your tail. If gratitude is good, appreciation is better. The mantra that happy dogs live by is said best by writer G.B. Stern: "Silent gratitude isn't much use to anyone."

The beauty of appreciation is that it makes everyone feel good, whether they are showing appreciation or receiving it. It turns everyday, ordinary events into special occasions. (A liver snap? For little old me? Oh, thank you! Thank you! Thank you!) Appreciation is also contagious, like a smile or a sneeze. If you've had a bad day at work, it's impossible to stay grumpy when your dog greets you at the door, bouncing up and down with appreciation for your safe return. Things don't look so bad all of a sudden, do they?

Appreciation also has an uncanny way of breaking down barriers. Whenever I score a piece of cheese, I do a little dance of happiness that charms my two-legged humans and weakens their resolve to give me "just this one little piece." Take my advice: A wee bit of appreciation will *always* get you more than just one little piece of cheese!

APPRECIATE THE MOMENT

Dogs are experts at appreciation because we live for the moment. When someone or something makes us happy, we drop whatever we are doing and share our joy with the world right away. It doesn't matter if up until then we've been having a bad day or if the future looks bleak—when something good comes along, we take a few moments to kick up our paws and celebrate.

It's pretty easy to be appreciative when things are going right. Appreciation becomes a lot more powerful when it seems like everything is going wrong. Appreciation protects our health and keeps us from going crazy.

Ironically, the most appreciative creatures are often the ones who've had the toughest breaks. Indeed, dogs who have been rescued from lives of abuse and neglect are often the most thankful, and will often show it with generous, sloppy licks and kisses for anyone with a kind word or soft touch. They remind humans to stop and appreciate the people and things in life that are good instead of focusing on the things that aren't.

Case Study:
Give a Dog a Bone

In the late 1990s, Corinne Dowling volunteered as a dog walker at San Francisco's Department of Animal Care & Control. She noticed a group of dogs who were kept isolated from the rest. Some of these "custody dogs" had been rescued from neglectful and cruel situations, and others were in legal limbo because their humans had been jailed or evicted. Dogs often spent weeks or months in their kennels waiting to be returned to their humans, adopted out, or, in the worst case, put down. Isolated from human contact, some of the dogs became bored and severely stressed.

One of the first custody dogs Corinne met was a starving shepherd mix named Lucky, who had been removed from an abusive situation but wasn't adjusting well to the shelter. As Lucky frantically paced back and forth in her kennel, Corinne spent hours with her to gain her trust and affection. When a loving family finally adopted Lucky, Corinne knew she had found her life's work. She started Give a Dog a Bone (GADAB), a nonprofit program to improve the quality of life for San Francisco's long-term shelter dogs while providing them with real world training and socialization.

To date, Corinne and her staff of volunteers have lavished exercise, affection, soft blankets and chew toys on more than 2,400 dogs. These are dogs like Pippin, who was brought in by a 13-year-old boy who was riding a city bus when he saw a group of men beating a puppy. The boy jumped off the bus, rescued the puppy and brought her to GADAB, where she was adopted. Amazingly, Pippin still loves humans and daily shows her appreciation by exuberantly wagging her tail.

Sadly, not all dogs are as fortunate as Lucky and Pippin, which makes direct dog care such an emotional, heart-wrenching job. The logistics of running a nonprofit enrichment program like GADAB aren't easy, either, and finding the financial support to keep the operation going is a constant battle. On more than one occasion, Corinne has had to take on part-time work to keep from closing the doors.

Despite the challenges, Corinne keeps going. What drives her? Appreciation. It's the appreciation she has for people who adopt custody dogs, and for people like the 13-year-old hero who did the right thing. It's the appreciation that she receives from the public and from animal welfare organizations like the ASPCA and the Animal Rescue Foundation. But most of all, it's the tail-wagging, tongue-licking appreciation that she gets back from her dogs and that reminds her why her work is important. *www.gadab.org*

Corinne's hard work proves that if you appreciate the things that are working instead of becoming discouraged by those that aren't, you can overcome huge hurdles and become a catalyst for change.

THOU SHALT NOT WHINE

Dogs don't lie, so I can't say that I never whine. There is always a legitimate reason for my complaining, though. For example, when my red rubber ball rolls under the fence into the neighbor's yard, I whine loudly until someone with long arms and opposable thumbs gets the hint and retrieves it for me. If my two-legged mom is tardy in feeding me my supper, I sit next to her desk at precisely 6:01 p.m. and let loose with a high-pitched howl.

That said, dogs don't hold a candle to humans in the complaint department. The weather's too hot, the coffee's cold, civility is dead and cable TV rates have increased at three times the rate of inflation (and that's just what the humans in my house are squawking about). It's a lot easier to kvetch about things that aren't working than it is to fix them. In fact, complaining has become such an ingrained habit that many of you don't even realize you are doing it, unlike dogs, who, as I've said, always have a reason. Unfortunately, complaining also feeds on itself. The average person complains between 15 and 30 times a day. Worse, as soon as one of you expresses dissatisfaction, the door is wide open for the rest of the pack to chime in.

What's all the whining about? Well, I think a lot of it has to do with "stuff." Humans spend an awful lot of time thinking about what they don't have instead of enjoying what they already do have. Personally, I don't own a lot of stuff—mostly because it's so much fun tearing things apart. Just ask my humans, who've replaced two dog beds, three sofa pillows, one comforter, dozens of rolls of toilet paper, a paperback book and a pair of swim goggles on my account (and one of those squishy pillows that are great fun until they burst and shoot out millions of magnetic microbeads that stick to your jowls and clog your nostrils).

Aside from the fun factor, I don't own a lot because dogs in general are minimalists. With less to worry about, we have a lot less to whine about. Our human friends, however, are drowning in their own junk. Does this explain why it's easier to spot a self-storage facility than it is to find a fire hydrant?

I may be a dog, but I'm not making this up. The United States has more than 50,000 self-storage facilities with 2.3 billion square feet of storage space. When I think of all the off-leash dog parks that could have been built and the land that could have been preserved, I want to howl.

What's really ridiculous is that the more stuff you humans have, the more you seem to complain. Apparently, stuff doesn't take up just physical space; it also occupies precious mindshare. Whether you want a lawn mower or a new living room sofa, humans have a dizzying number of options to choose from. Gas or electric? Leather or upholstered? Once you've figured that out, you have to bring the thing home, find space for it and take care of it. Then when it breaks, wears out or gets clogged with dog hair, you have to find a way to get rid of it. Just thinking about all the steps involved is exhausting.

My advice? Clean out your doghouse. Simplify, streamline and unclutter. Learn to be more appreciative by focusing on what you have instead of complaining about what you don't. And, if you do catch yourself starting to whine, give yourself a slap on the paw (just kidding, but not really).

Case Study:
A Complaint-Free World
....

Will Bowen, an animal-loving minister in Kansas City, Mo., lets his staff bring their dogs to work and encourages church members to bring their pets to his office when they come for a visit. Unlike their humans, however, the animals never complain.

In fact, Will was so sick of all the complaining going on in his church that he decided to do something about it. In 2006, he started handing out purple rubber wristbands and asked his congregants to switch the bracelet from one wrist to the other whenever they caught themselves whining about something. The idea was to get people to go 21 days without switching wrists, after which they would ideally have formed a new, "noncomplaining" habit.

All of a sudden, people who didn't think they were whiners found they were moving the bracelet 10 times a day. Others stopped talking until they figured out how to have conversations that didn't involve complaining. In the time since, Bowen's nonreligious nonprofit organization, A Complaint Free World, has sent nearly 8 million purple rubber bracelets to people in more than 106 countries. The organization's goal is to help 60 million people, or 1 percent of the world's human population, redirect their words and thoughts to become complaint-free. It's such a fabulous and simple concept, a dog should have thought of it! *www.acomplaintfreeworld.org*

DEVELOP AN ATTITUDE OF GRATITUDE

I'm grateful for every day with my humans, but some days are easier than others. When I have a stomachache because I've eaten something I wasn't supposed to, or my plans to go to the beach get scrapped because my humans have to work, I need to take a few seconds to think about all the other things that I am grateful for. Fortunately, I don't have to think very long. Here's my starter list of things to be grateful for:

- My four-legged pals at dog day care
- A brand-spanking-new tennis ball
- A dog collar that doesn't itch
- A fluffy dog pillow in every room of the house
- Crumbs on the floor
- Getting a clean bill of health from the vet
- A water bowl that's always full
- Sun puddles
- Dad letting me jump on the furniture
- Mom not catching me jump on the furniture

I know that some humans keep daily "gratitude journals" to write down the things they are grateful for every day. This seems like a pretty good idea, because humans who are grateful for what they have are a lot like dogs: They are more alert, have higher levels of energy, exercise more and sleep better. They are also more likely to achieve their personal and professional goals than people who are less grateful in their daily lives.

Of course, if my own humans are any example, most gratitude journals probably end up in drawers and behind nightstands, where they collect dust bunnies. (Why are they called dust bunnies, anyway? They don't have whiskers and they don't put up a chase.) I prefer to live my gratitude by dragging my own two-leggeds out for a daily "gratitude walk" around the neighborhood. While I sniff around bushes and stare down squirrels, they get some quality time to reflect on all the things they are grateful for.

In fact, I suggest that *all* humans take their dogs out on daily gratitude walks. As I said in Chapter 2, if you don't live with a dog of your own, then volunteer as a dog walker at your local shelter, walk with a friend or walk yourself. While you are walking, think about everything you are grateful for, even if you can't think of anything beyond the basics like food and shelter. Nothing's too small, or too elemental, to be taken for granted.

PUPPY APPRECIATION LESSONS

As a dog, I make a point of showing my appreciation all the time, and I'm often surprised that humans, well, don't. In fact, I'll bet that some humans say "good dog" more than they say "thank you" to their family, friends, bosses, clients, co-workers or employees. If gratitude is good for our own health and happiness, then passing it along to others in the form of appreciation is a win-win for everyone. So what's the deal?

My guess is that some humans feel awkward about showing their appreciation for others. They think it's too "mushy," or they don't think it's their job or place to say thank you. Maybe they think the other person already knows that he or she is appreciated—a mistake a dog never makes! Or maybe people just haven't been taught good manners. That, at least, is something that can be cured by going to puppy kindergarten.

This may sound silly, but it isn't. The idea behind puppy kindergarten is to build up a dog's energy and confidence, motivate him or her to work harder, and create a strong and rewarding human-animal bond. It's all about positive reinforcement, and that applies to both humans and dogs.

Acknowledging someone else's efforts and actions builds their confidence and gains their trust. If you're too busy or too important to thank people for their efforts, you're also making an impression—an impression that's pretty much like lifting your leg on your neighbor's new rosebush (and yes, this is a not-so-subtle hint to the cheeky cocker spaniel who lives down the street).

So what does puppy kindergarten teach us about showing appreciation to others, whether savvy dogs or almost-savvy people? Here are some of the lessons I learned.

Make It Personal

In puppy class, humans reward their four-legged fur babies with the things that mean the most to them. Some pups like hot dogs, others like liver snaps and the really smart ones will do anything for cheese (yes, please!). Some dogs (weirdly) aren't motivated by food at all and respond best to squeaky toys or praise. Whether dealing with dogs or humans, appreciation isn't a one-size-fits-all proposition. Find ways to say thank you that are meaningful for the person (or pup) being rewarded.

Be Specific

Well-trained pups are rewarded for specific, desired behaviors. Merely showing up at obedience class doesn't warrant a treat, but performing a "down stay" on command does. Show people that you are paying attention to what they do and tell them exactly what you are thanking them for. This lets them know they are making a difference and gives them the confidence and encouragement to continue doing so.

Time It Right

When it comes to training a puppy, timing is everything. There's no point in rewarding or scolding a dog after the fact, because he or she won't associate the behavior with the reward or reprimand. What's the hardest part about training a dog? Keeping cool when you come home to a pile of shredded sofa pillows (you're a gem, Mom). Fortunately, humans have better memories than their dogs. If you've neglected to recognize someone for a job well done, go back and acknowledge them as soon as possible. In the future, show your appreciation right away and don't wait for "designated" days like birthdays, holidays or annual performance reviews.

Be Sincere

Don't be stingy with praise, but don't overdo it, either. It's hard to hold back praise with adorable puppies, especially boxers, but if every other phrase is "Good puppy!" your dog won't know the difference between genuine appreciation and regular conversation. People also have an annoying habit of throwing dozens of "thank-yous" and "thanks" into their daily conversations; these are general pleasantries instead of genuine expressions of appreciation (start listening for it and right away you'll hear what I mean). Save your thank-yous for when you really mean them and they are deserved.

PUTTING PAWS TO PAPER

I'll admit that the famous boxer kidney-bean dance isn't appropriate for most people, unless they happen to be a boxer or just incredibly limber. However, if someone does something nice for you, does a good job at work, gives you a business referral or takes time out of their busy day to meet with you, you should acknowledge their effort and express your appreciation in a genuine way. This might sound like obvious advice, but I've observed enough human behavior to know that this sort of personal and professional consideration is surprisingly rare. On the plus side, it means you'll stand out from the crowd, and people will remember you.

So what should you do? Phone calls and personal visits are nice, but nothing beats a good old-fashioned thank-you note. And while an electronic "thank-you" is always better than nothing at all, a handwritten note is much more powerful. In fact, humans seem to go gaga over them. I know, because every afternoon at 2 p.m. I saunter to the front door to wait for the mailman, who, honest to dog, wears a pith helmet and Bermuda shorts no matter what the weather. Safari outfit aside, the mailman doesn't usually deliver anything interesting. Yet among the bills and the junk mail there is an occasional surprise: a personal, handwritten note. Suddenly, both my mom and dad want to open the envelope and see what's inside.

As much as humans love getting personalized notes through the traditional mail system, however, very few bother to send them out themselves. That's a shame, because for the price of a greeting card and a first-class stamp, you automatically differentiate yourself from the rest of the pack. My advice is to make it a regular habit by setting aside a time each week to write a few notes of appreciation. Don't write an essay, either. You just need three to five well-written lines to let someone know you are thinking about them and they are not just a bunch of bits and bytes in your contact management system.

Case Study:
The Packards

A few years ago, Jim and Sherry Packard rescued a cocker spaniel named Gracie. She came to them with multiple issues, both behavioral and medical. Still, "Gracie was full of life and taught us to live in the moment and enjoy everyday," says Sherry.

Unfortunately, Gracie developed serious complications after having surgery to repair both her knees. Things were looking very bleak when, against all odds, Gracie awoke from a coma and began making a slow yet steady recovery. Naturally, the Packards were overjoyed. They also knew that the financial obligations for Gracie's recovery would be steep, so they were doubly surprised to receive a bill that was thousands of dollars less than what they had expected. Amazingly, the veterinarian had covered the majority of the costs out of his own pocket. Why the good fortune? The Packards attribute it to a card campaign that "touched the doctor's heart."

For five straight days, the Packards had sent cards with personalized messages and pictures to the veterinary hospital, bringing laughter and smiles to the nurses, doctors and office staff. As Jim recalls, the first three cards were addressed directly to Gracie, with sayings such as "Sorry you're going through such a ruff time" and "We're thinking about you." The veterinary staff took turns reading the cards to Gracie and showing her the pictures of her family that were printed inside.

The fourth and fifth cards were mailed directly to Gracie's nurses and veterinarian, thanking them for their continuing care and concern for their dog. One card, with Gracie's picture on the front, said, "Thank you for taking care of me," and another offered a preemptive canine apology: "Sorry if I'm not a model patient, but I don't like being away from my parents."

"We didn't do anything above and beyond," explained Sherry. "We just wanted to say thank you to everyone who took such good care of Gracie. In the process, we learned that when you give unexpected and heartfelt gratitude, you get love and generosity in return."

Sadly, Gracie died of kidney failure in July 2008. But her story still teaches people the value of expressing their heartfelt appreciation for others: When you show your appreciation, good things come back to you.

A CLOSING THOUGHT

Earlier I mentioned Jenny Walker, my two-legged mom's exercise instructor, who always ends her high-intensity classes by telling students to feel a sense of appreciation for what they've just accomplished. According to Jenny, "Appreciation keeps my heart and mind positive and forces me to think of others instead of myself. It puts me on a higher frequency and lets me care for others on a larger scale. It also reminds me how lucky I am to have my health, my family, my dog—and how precious they all are to me."

Good words to live by, right?

BELLA'S SOUND BITES

- Don't just be grateful—show it. Appreciation is gratitude in action, and it makes everyone feel good.

- Appreciate the moment. When something good happens, take a moment out of your busy life to kick up your paws and celebrate.

- Simplify, streamline and unclutter; focus on what you have instead of whining about what you don't.

- Acknowledge other people's efforts and actions; everyone wants to feel like they are making a difference.

....
Chapter 9

Play:
Stop and Eat
the Roses

We do not stop playing because we grow old, we grow
old because we stop playing.

– Benjamin Franklin

I think we are drawn to dogs because they are the
uninhibited creatures we might be if we weren't
certain we knew better.

– George Bird Evans

When I was a puppy (OK, until I was about 2 years old),
I just couldn't get enough of my two-legged mom's prize-
winning rosebushes. They tasted so great! As soon as the
beautiful blooms popped up in the late spring, I'd chop
them off and run crazy circles around the yard with my
ears flopping in the wind and the soft, velvety rose petals

flying out of my mouth. My mom would sometimes join in the fun, too, by chasing me around the yard.

Since then, I've outgrown my taste for rosebuds and most of the garden has recovered (not everything is as tough as a boxer). These days, I prefer to chew on my mom's cherry tomato plants. But back then, eating the roses was pure, unadulterated fun—and definitely worth the occasional thorn.

You see, boxers love to play. We're a silly breed, despite our serious appearance. In fact, humans call us the clowns of the canine world because we are so happy-go-lucky. Forget about prey drive, we're all about the play drive! The only downside is that without an appropriate outlet for fun, we'll usually stir some up on our own—by shredding your evil couch pillows or trimming your unruly rosebushes, for example.

Still, despite our reputations as party animals, we aren't the only dogs who love to play. Police and guide dogs balance work with fun to keep from burning out, and anyone visiting a dog training center will see brightly colored play structures, plastic kiddie pools, agility equipment and tug toys. These tools help hardworking dogs burn off excess energy while stimulating their minds and senses and improving their physical coordination and confidence.

WHAT HAPPENED TO PLAYTIME?

So what's going on with you humans? What happened to play? Sure, you have to exercise, but play is a lot more than that. The crazy thing is that you are working more than ever, thanks to all the "time-saving" devices that let you log on from anywhere at any time. Your gadgets are getting sleeker and smarter, but they're also piling on the pressure to get more work done, and done faster. As much as I'd like to think you are all as eager to get home and walk your dog as you are to check your smartphones and PDAs, I know too many people who spend their off-hours answering work-related e-mails and sending messages from wherever they happen to be. A dog on a 6-foot leash has a lot more room to wiggle than a human who is tied to the office via an invisible digital leash. (Which, if you ask me, is a lot like the retractable kind that Mom and Dad use when we go hiking in the woods. One minute you're free, and then—whammo!—you get reeled back in.)

The worst part is that you spend a lot of your off-hours— really, it's your leisure time, not off time—in front of the television. To be perfectly honest, I'd probably watch more television than I do right now if I could figure out how to wrap my paws around the remote control. But still, the average human spends nearly five hours per day in front of the TV. Five hours per day! Who plays outside with their dogs anymore? It's no surprise that so many of you feel like you've been sucked dry while your adorable dogs are bored out of their minds and bouncing off the walls.

Another problem is that humans think play is the opposite of work. Play is something that they squeeze into their schedules after they've satisfied all the duties and obligations of daily life.

Now compare that mind-set to a dog's way of thinking. We see play in an entirely different light. For us, play *is* one of the duties and obligations of daily life. It's an instinctive ritual. It's a way to discover our surroundings, burn off energy and recharge our batteries. In fact, play is how all animals grow mentally and physically, from dogs to dolphins to yellow-bellied marmots. When it comes to play, humans have a lot to learn from the animal world.

Case Study:
The Evolution of Play

In 1992, photographer Norbert Rosing captured a series of images in Churchill, Manitoba, that showed a 1,200-pound male polar bear appearing out of the blue and approaching a tethered husky. Instead of engaging in a deadly showdown, however, the bear and dog faced each other and began to wrestle and play. Every night for more than a week, the polar bear returned to roughhouse with the husky until the ice froze over and the polar bear left to hunt for seals.

According to Stuart Brown, MD, founder and president of the National Institute of Play, the rough-and-tumble play of the polar bear and the husky is not unlike the behavior at a preschool playground. To adults, the scene is chaotic and sometimes frightening: Kids are screaming, squealing and taking swings at each other. Yet what looks like anarchy on the playground is really just a way for kids to find their place in the pack. It's how they learn to use their natural talents to resolve issues—whether through physical strength, verbal reasoning, creativity or imagination.

Brown says that humans and animals who have been deprived of play often lack the tools to deal with a rapidly changing world. They are inflexible, don't socialize well, are less likely to seek out new and different things and are more likely to be depressed. Why? Because free play helps people develop complex problem-solving skills and makes it easier for them to adapt to changing circumstances. Play builds empathy and trust and prevents violent behavior: Once a child learns what it feels like to be whacked hard with a toy, he or she is less likely to whack back.

www.nifplay.org

Of course, a playful life includes taking risks. If you eat roses, you will occasionally get stuck by thorns. That's just the way it is. The real challenge for most humans is to find a balance between safety and spontaneity. This is especially true for parents. It doesn't matter if your babies have a head of hair or a coat of fur—they will *always* find a way to play. It is, after all, essential to the evolution of the species, whether you are a polar bear, a husky or a human.

PLAY LIKE A DOG

A dog will tell you that any time is a good time for a playdate—as long as the other dog (or human) is in the mood to play. In fact, that's why dogs have developed their own social protocol for inviting someone to play: We stick our butts in the air, plop our front legs on the ground, prick up our ears and give a big happy grin.

Humans call this maneuver a "play bow." It's our way of persuading someone to come and join us in stirring up some fun. It's also the way we keep a play session going—for example, if we get a little too rambunctious with another pup, we'll play-bow to say, "Sorry, buddy! Let's keep playing." You're not likely to see a dog play-bow to a television set or a computer monitor, either. That's because play is our way of connecting with *real* people, *real* dogs and *real* tennis balls. You know—the things in life that are most important.

Of course, dogs don't expect humans to stand up from their desks and stick their tails and ears in the air. That's too silly, even for a boxer. But I don't think there's a dog who'll disagree with me when I say that the world would be a much calmer place if more humans took figurative play bows by getting up, taking a look around them and figuring out how to bring back playtime.

But what exactly is play? The way I see things, it's not play if it involves a keypad or a screen or a remote control. Play is also not about having free time and doing nothing with it. That's called downtime, something we all need once in a while to keep from going insane. At its most basic, play is a toe-to-tail sensory experience: a bout of tug-of-war, a round of hopscotch, a game of tag or hide-and-go-seek. It's hot, sweaty fun that gets the heart pumping and sends blood to the hippocampus, the part of the brain responsible for long-term memory and verbal learning.

Play can also be a state of mind. It's a way to challenge the brain and recharge the soul, whether you're listening to a concert, studying a new language or training for canine agility. And even though the opportunities for play are limitless, they don't just drop out of the sky. Humans tend to forget that play is a process that takes practice, planning and a healthy sense of curiosity.

THE BEGINNER'S EYE

There is a saying: "In the beginner's eye there are many possibilities, in the expert's eyes there are few." Fortunately, dogs see themselves as perpetual beginners. Dogs see everything as new, so everything has possibilities—and it's usually about play. A dog can find something fun and interesting in a scene that he or she has seen a hundred times before, thanks to a healthy sense of wonder and curiosity.

Kyoko Nakayama knows this, too. She's a dog trainer and professional photographer in Hawaii who compares her creativity and sense of adventure to the way her dogs walk when they are off leash: "Dogs that have been down the same path a hundred times will still stop to sniff whatever catches their fancy, as if they've never been there before. Likewise, as a photographer I don't think in a linear fashion. I don't plan my photo shoots too far in advance, and I photograph whatever inspires me that day."

Kyoko says that her dogs teach her to stay curious and playful, and to be less cerebral in the way she approaches things. They keep her excited about photography, and excited about the world around her.

Dogs also aren't afraid to play because we aren't obsessed with perfection. Frankly, we don't care if we have natural talent for something or what other people think about our abilities, as long as we're having fun. Take the example of my blogging buddy Chef, a boxer in Canada who competes in dog shows and fancies himself an artist. Chef takes a break from the pressures of the show ring by building elaborate stick sculptures in his backyard. He never gets tired of looking for cool new sticks that he can whittle with his teeth and add to his latest chef-d'oeuvre (CHEF-d'oeuvre, get it? I told you boxers were funny!). Although Chef's talent for modern art is questionable, sculpting makes him happy and keeps him energized when he's not in the show ring.

Another example of beginner's eye is from Anthony Sandberg, a two-legged friend of Mom and Dad's who runs OCSC SAILING, one of the country's best sailing schools. To put himself in his students' shoes and remember what it's like to be a beginning sailor, Anthony has developed a unique life plan: Learn two brand new activities each year and "practice" the art of play. The activities may have little in common besides the fact that they attract other curious, creative people. Over the past decade he's taken up surfing, Spanish, kiteboarding, yoga, open-water swimming, meditation, tango dancing, horse whispering and acting. According to Anthony, play is a chance to become a student again. It's a way to open the door to new ways of learning and teaching and to connect with the people around you.

The lesson for humans is this: Pick an activity that fires up your creativity and challenges you. It doesn't matter what it is or whether you are particularly good at it. The point is that as soon as you stop thinking about play as a luxury and start considering it a necessity, you'll find a way to make it a part of your daily life.

FAIR PLAY—RULES OF THE GAME

Dogs have the good sense to recognize that playtime is supposed to be fun for everyone. This is why I can rough-house with my two-legged dad one minute, yet play very gently with my little sister the next. For the same reason, you'll never find a team of German shepherds throwing balls at a pack of Pomeranians (otherwise known to two-legged schoolchildren everywhere as the dreaded game of dodgeball).

That's not to say that a German shepherd and a Pomeranian can't be playmates. On the contrary, canines of all sizes, shapes and strengths can play nicely together by periodically reversing roles—meaning that one minute the German shepherd is on his back and the next minute it's the Pomeranian's turn. Switching between dominant and submissive postures is a dog's way of keeping things even, of making sure that everyone's having fun and that the party doesn't end with somebody going home in tears.

Dogs use role reversal with their two-legged humans, too. For example, once or twice a day I like to nudge my officemates away from their computers and into the outdoors for a game of keep-away. The game starts with them tossing the ball to each other while I pretend to try to steal it. After the ball has passed back and forth a dozen times or so, I make my move: a dramatic, midair interception. Suddenly, the game becomes exciting again as the humans run after me. Thanks to the role reversal, everyone gets a chance to feel in charge and the game stays fun.

Of course, there are some dogs who just don't play well with others. I know, because I've run into a few of them at the local dog park. Likewise, there are humans who don't play well with others. For the most part, it's simply because they don't know *how* to. That's because humans look for business mentors, fitness mentors and even relationship mentors, but relatively few think about finding mentors who can teach them how to make the most out of play.

Let me give you a personal example. My favorite place to play is on the beach. In fact, I love it so much that my two-legged humans plan some of their vacations around beaches where I can run off leash and chase my little red rubber ball in and out of the waves. I'm a lucky dog who has a lot of fun, and I know my humans like watching me run figure eights in the sand as much as I like running them. Which is proof that watching other people at play can be a source of joy and learning, too.

And yet the water used to scare me. That was before I met Norman, the underwear-eating, water-loving chocolate Labrador who took me under his wing. Norman taught me how to play in the water. He showed me how to bury my ball in the sand and how to clean it off with a quick dip in the waves. He taught me how to hold a ball underwater with my paw and then let it go so that it shoots straight up into the air. He convinced me that getting my nostrils wet isn't the end of the world.

I'm not saying that when a rogue wave washes my ball out of my comfort zone I don't rely on Norman's chivalry—and superior swimming skills—to rescue it for me. But thanks to my play mentor Norman, I'm as comfortable around water as any boxer can be expected to be. So how do you find your own Norman? Well, unlike other mentors, play mentors aren't assigned or hired. They need to be discovered—which is relatively easy to do, as they're the ones having the most fun!

FOR DOG'S SAKE, PLAY

I can be a pretty persuasive boxer; some people might even say that I can be a pest (although these people are wrong). But I'm not much different from every other dog who tries to get his or her humans to get up, get out and play. Still, I know there are plenty of harried humans who feel they have no time to stop and smell the roses—much less taste them. But playtime is important for physical, mental and emotional well-being. Breaking up the workday with a little bit of play will reduce stress and contribute to a longer and healthier life. And let's be totally honest here: Nobody goes to their deathbed wishing they had worked more and played less.

So grab a leash and go out to play with your dog. You'll make your loyal friend very happy and add years to his life—not to mention your own.

BELLA'S SOUND BITES

- Put away the gadgets and gizmos and play like a dog, where play is a full-body sensory experience that connects you to the real world and makes other people happy, too.

- Don't think of play as an escape from daily life, but rather an important part of learning and development. If you don't play, you don't grow.

- Sniff out new and different ways to play. A healthy sense of curiosity is what makes life interesting.

- Make time for play, practice how to play—and look for playful role models to show you the way.

Chapter 10

Presence:
Cheese the Moment

The secret of health for both mind and body is
not to mourn for the past, worry about the future,
or anticipate troubles, but to live in the present
moment wisely and earnestly.

– Buddha

My dog is usually pleased with what I do,
because she is not infected with the concept
of what I "should" be doing.

– Lonzo Idolswine

What is it that makes you live in the moment? What
makes time stand still? For me, it's cheese. Cheese makes
me weak in the knees. Sure, some dogs have a talent for
sniffing out the tiniest traces of drugs or dynamite, but my
antenna is always tuned to cheese. Nothing, and I mean
nothing, can muffle the unmistakable rustle of someone
unwrapping a Camembert or unzipping a package of

shredded mozzarella (not even the racket my dad makes as he bangs pots and pans around the kitchen like he's trying to wake a sleeping dog—or my mom).

Seriously, I'll do anything it takes to sink my crooked little boxer teeth into a piece of cheese. I don't care whether it's a block of cheap cheddar or a wedge of the finest French Gruyere. I roll it around on my tongue like it's the best thing I have ever tasted in my whole life. Why? Because at that exact moment, it *is* the best thing I have ever tasted in my whole life! I don't compare it with yesterday's morsel, and I don't worry about whether there'll be any left for tomorrow. I clear my head and focus my attention on the delectable chunk of dairy that is in front of me *right here and right now.*

TURN DOWN THE VOLUME

OK, so not everybody loves cheese as much as I do. The point is that dogs throw themselves into the present and embrace it for all it's worth. I'm not saying that we don't learn from the past or look ahead to the future (believe me, I know well ahead of time when my mom has signed me up for a day of fun at dog day care). Yet living in the here and now is just something that comes naturally to us. It is part of our inherent dogness and why some people refer to us as "furry Buddhas."

On the contrary, too many humans spend their lives rehashing the past or fretting about the future. Granted, it's a hard cycle to break. The world we live in is jam-packed with obligations and distractions. On a typical workday, for example, my two-legged dad shifts between sending e-mails, making phone calls and running to appointments. My mom jumps from one activity to another and races from thought to thought until it's hard to tell where one stops and the other begins. They zip about in a whir of activity that gives new meaning to the term "monkey mind" and makes even a boxer's head spin.

For all their hyperactivity, my humans aren't very different from their peers. Humans tend to look at success as a destination, certain they'll be successful when they reach some specific goal. Their eyes are usually fixed on the horizon, but from what I can tell, that horizon keeps shifting. Looking forward is excellent, but people seem so obsessed with the future that they sometimes miss what's right under their own noses.

Take it from me, people: To live mindfully and in the moment, you need to let go and loosen up. Stop being a slave to your schedule. Turn down the volume on the chatter going through your head—you know, all the "could'ves," "should'ves" and "would'ves" that cause you so much anxiety and guilt. Instead, take note of all the wonderful things that are happening around you. Embrace the moment and go with the flow.

Easier said than done, right? Well, yes and no. Stop overthinking things. Be aware of your thoughts, but don't get lost in them. If it's a bright and sunny summer day and you feel like sticking your head out the car window, then stick your head out the car window (as long as it's safe, of course). Don't stop to think about all the reasons you shouldn't. In the time it takes to imagine what other people will think or worry about messing up your hair, the window of opportunity will have closed. Instead, do it because it's fun. Do it because you can. Do it because your dog wouldn't give it a second thought.

SHARPEN YOUR SENSES

Dogs savor every minute of life to its fullest, especially the things we can see, taste or, better yet, smell. In fact, if a dog can't sniff something from top to bottom, it's probably not very interesting. But how many humans chew their food without tasting it? Read a book without understanding a sentence? Listen to a speech without remembering a word? There's not a dog on the planet who believes that this is the way to get the most out of life.

Unfortunately, humans aren't wired to experience the world through their senses like a dog does, but that's no excuse for not trying—just ask any kid. That's why my favorite walking partner is my two-legged little sister. She stops to smell every plant and every flower and doesn't tug at my leash when I linger over a blade of grass. She gathers crab apples and pinecones and lets me eat them out of her hands. We stop every few feet to listen to the sounds of passing birds, squirrels and motorcycles. It takes us a while to get down the block, but we're convinced that we live on the most exciting street in the whole world.

If you won't stop to smell everything that crosses your path, at least keep your senses sharp by doing some of the things I like to do:

- Follow a bumblebee with your eyes. Observe every little thing it does until it zigzags out of sight. Just don't follow it with your teeth—trust me, you'll end up with a swollen lip and a sore ego.
- Experiment with different foods. In the summer, I like to harvest tomatoes right off the vine. When it's cold and rainy, I prefer to stay inside and surf the kitchen counters (sweet potatoes, yum; kale, yuck).
- Perk up your ears (and for God's sake, take out those annoying ear buds before you ruin your hearing for good). Tune in to the sounds that nobody else hears. Be warned, however: If you do this exercise in the middle of the night, you will freak out your roommates.
- Throw yourself into a puddle and feel the mud squish between your paws. Nudge earthworms with your nose. And when you're good and dirty, roll around on the cool, smooth leather couch when nobody's looking. Feels heavenly, doesn't it?

Fortunately, you don't have to be a (naughty) dog to immerse yourself in an experience. You don't have to be a rock star or a celebrity to live a colorful life, either. In fact, you don't have to be anybody but yourself as long as you tune in to your senses and start savoring life instead of rushing through it at breakneck speed.

LOOK PAST YOUR OWN NOSE

If it seems like dogs are at one with the universe, it's because we are. Mindful of our own thoughts and actions, we look past our own snouts and connect with the dogs and people that surround us. I guess that's what makes us such excellent companions to humans of all races, religions and abilities: We motivate people to become more involved, or more present, in their own lives and in the lives of others.

Case Study:
Delta Society

Laird Goodman is a doctor of veterinary medicine and a member of the board of directors at the Delta Society, an international, nonprofit organization whose Pet Partners Program trains and screens volunteers and their pets for visiting animal programs in hospitals, nursing homes, rehabilitation centers, schools and other facilities.

According to Dr. Goodman, humans spend over 80 percent of their time worrying about the future or obsessing over the past. Part of the healing power of animals is that they help humans focus beyond themselves, saving them from unhealthy patterns and putting them in tune with their own selves: "With a pet in our lives, we are forced to focus on the here and now. Our animals not only need us for basics like food and water, but also for companionship and love."

A connection with animals is essential to the physical and emotional health of humans. Dr. Goodman points to scientific studies that demonstrate that having a pet can reduce blood pressure, lower stress levels and decrease pain (wouldn't it be great if doctors prescribed pet interactions as often as they prescribe drugs?). This has partly to do with the activation of "feel good" hormones when humans pet an animal.

"The physical act of petting or hugging an animal helps keep us calm, relaxes us, and decreases our sense of loneliness," notes Dr. Goodman. He suggests that humans who have a relationship with a pet are more inclined to interact with others, including strangers. "Animals guarantee social contact and open up whole new worlds. In a sense, they keep us human and remind us that we have just one life to live." *www.deltasociety.org*

Anyone who's ever hugged an animal knows about the healing power of touch. Dogs know it, too. We aren't above throwing ourselves at someone's feet after a day of hard work to ask for ear scratches and belly rubs. We aren't afraid to squeeze ourselves onto someone's lap for reassurance when we hear the rumble of a thunderstorm.

So why is it that people are so clumsy when it comes to reaching out to touch each other? I suppose that there are some people (cat lovers, I'm sure) who might consider our behavior pushy or needy, but dogs know what we're doing. We teach humans how to reach out and give love and how to ask for physical affection and attention in return, in all of its satisfying, slobbery and embarrassing glory. Want to look past yourself, live in the glorious moment and feel connected to your dogs and to other people? Just reach out and touch someone.

HEART OVER HEAD

Humans are an enthusiastic bunch. The people I meet have as much zeal for making things bigger, better, faster and stronger as I have for eating cheese. They have the technology and the skills to do it, too. But not everything in life needs improving. To truly live in the moment you have to accept that some things are just fine the way that they are.

The same goes for our relationships with other people. Look up the definition of "unconditional love." If you don't see a picture of a dog, you should. That's because a dog will love you no matter what you look like, what you wear or what you do. It doesn't matter if you have a job, a house or a car—or whether you buy your four-legged friend a $1,500 designer dog collar or one from the dollar store. (And believe me, you'll be a lot happier when he rolls around in a mud puddle wearing the dollar collar!) A dog will never judge you, and we don't expect you to become someone other than who you already are.

Indeed, dogs are excellent at giving unconditional love because we don't have unrealistic, romantic ideas about what makes someone "perfect." The truth is that nobody is perfect. We all have moments where we snap at the people around us. We all have bad habits that drive other people crazy. Remember Gracie the cocker spaniel from an earlier chapter? Jim and Sherry Packard adopted the rescue dog despite her challenges. Fortunately, they refused to give up on her. "We made a commitment to Gracie and accepted her for who she was," explained Sherry.

Although Gracie eventually adjusted to life with the Packards, she continued to channel her nervous energy by chewing. Gracie chewed her way through several crates and ate hundreds of dollars' worth of Jim's leather shoes, plus a few pairs of Sherry's favorite sandals. And yet, says Sherry, "Gracie taught us to lighten up. She taught us to live in the moment and take things one day at a time. She helped us learn patience, forgiveness and tolerance. She also taught us to be more careful with our shoes!"

You see, that's the thing about dogs. No matter how much mischief we cause, most humans are willing to look past our mistakes, problems and quirks. We help people focus on the moment and in the process we teach them the art of forgiveness. So while I excuse my two-legged companions for their annoying tendency to hog the living room couch, they don't hold a grudge when I wake them up at 5 a.m. (which I like to do by sneaking up to their bed and staring at them like one of those creepy Egyptian dogs who accompanied their masters to the underworld, wherever that is). Besides, as the saying goes, dogs who live in glass doghouses shouldn't throw bones.

Need another reason to stay rooted in the present? By accepting situations for what they are—not how they got that way or how to keep them from happening again—we can jump in with all four paws and start making a difference. Surely you've heard the expression "it all happened so fast that I didn't even have time to think"? The irony is that to be truly mindful, we occasionally need to shut off our heads and act with our hearts.

Case Study:
The Pongo Fund

As a busy and successful entrepreneur, Larry Chusid had a lot on his mind when he drove through Portland, Ore., in 2007 and noticed two humans camping with their dogs underneath a bridge. It was around Thanksgiving, and Larry's dog, Pongo, a canine gourmet with a preference for pot roast and gravy, had recently passed away at the ripe old age of 18.

Thinking about Pongo, Larry suddenly decided to stop. He asked the homeless men if there was anything he could do to help. They said they'd be eating Thanksgiving dinner at a nearby shelter, but that their dogs, Jackson and Jewels, were hungry. The homeless shelters around town rarely had any pet food, and the men often shared what little they had with their dogs. They were all hungry.

Larry later returned to the makeshift campsite with dog treats, dog beds and high-quality, nutritious kibble for Jackson and Jewels. The Pongo Fund was born. Over the next two years, Larry distributed more than 100,000 pet meals to Portland's homeless and transitional communities, where people often choose to feed their pets before themselves. "Sadly, 'living on the edge' has become a daily ritual for many people," explains Larry. "The Pongo Fund doesn't differentiate between people who live indoors and those that live outdoors. Our mission is to provide high-quality dog and cat food for the animals of anyone in honest need."

In 2009, Larry opened Portland's first pet food bank for families who might otherwise be forced to give up or abandon their pets because they can't afford to feed them. With the help of its generous suppliers, The Pongo Fund Pet Food Bank now donates more than 50,000 quality meals each month for starving family pets that might have nothing else to eat—nearly a million meals so far. The food bank keeps beloved pets well fed and out of shelters, and keeps families together during a time when all they have is each other. *www.thepongofund.org*

Larry Chusid hadn't planned to establish a community pet food bank when he stopped his car that day in 2007. Yet he saw an immediate need and decided to do something about it. Today, he keeps thousands of family pets from starving. For Larry and the volunteers at The Pongo Fund Pet Food Bank, the circumstances that bring people through the door don't matter. They might be millionaires facing foreclosure, white-collar workers who've recently been laid off, or seniors and students who are having trouble making ends meet. All that matters is that they need help right away. In return, they get food for their pets and a spark of hope to make it through another day.

ONE LIFE TO LIVE, OR NINE LIVES ARE JUST FOR CATS

Dogs may not live by their watches, but we know that every minute of every day is precious, and there is always something new to discover. Indeed, this book is long over-due because I tend to get distracted by all the magical, wonderful things that happen in the here and now—an unexpected ray of sunshine in the middle of a rainy day, a roast chicken left unattended on the kitchen counter or a squirrel that sets me off on the next great chase.

Speaking of chasing squirrels, I'm watching the neigh-borhood cats through my window as I write this final chapter. As much as I like to terrorize them, I also respect and admire their capacity to live entirely in the present. Monty, the neighborhood tough cat who looks like a cross between a Siamese and a raccoon, is currently stalking our common enemy.

Monty's leaps are powerful, and he's a fluid and grace-ful runner. He's working up a sweat, but he's also hav-ing fun—in fact, I swear he's got a grin on his face. At this moment, his whole world revolves around chasing the squirrel. Sure, I could shake things up by charging outside and annoying him, but Monty is doing an outstanding job pursuing our mutual foe. Besides, he once nearly got flattened by a speeding SUV, and I don't want him run-ning into the street. I secretly respect that focused feline and would be sad if he weren't around (although I'll never admit it to him and will deny it vehemently if questioned).

The bottom line is that Monty, along with every other animal on the planet, has much to teach humans about the power of living fully in the present. We all have one life to live. We are all just a tiny part of a much bigger picture—one that doesn't revolve around us, and where everyone and everything is interconnected. For us, life is about collecting experiences instead of things. It's about living fully in the present and loving every little moment for what it's worth.

I think humans should start living this way every single day, all day long.

Ready. Set. Live!

BELLA'S SOUND BITES

• Seize the opportunities that are under your nose right now, instead of digging around in the past or sniffing at the future.

• Loosen up. Ignore the "could'ves," "should'ves" and "would'ves" and go with the flow.

• Savor life with your senses. Slow down and tune in to the wonderful world around you.

• Pass along the gifts of friendship, forgiveness and compassion. The best way to be present in your own life is to be present in the lives of others.

Every Dog Has Her Day

Balance, peace, and joy are the fruit of a successful life.
It starts with recognizing your talents and finding ways
to serve others by using them.

– Thomas Kinkade

In order to really enjoy a dog, one doesn't merely try to
train him to be semi human. The point of it is to open
oneself to the possibility of becoming partly a dog.

– Edward Hoagland

I like to think that I have an instinctive and evolutionary advantage when it comes to living a well-balanced life. I build relationships by wagging my tail more than my tongue. I'm excited to give new things a try and resilient enough to bounce back if they don't work out. I blend work with fun and have a zest for living that doesn't revolve around shiny gadgets and beeping gizmos.

Keep in mind that I'm not a know-it-all. I'm anything but the perfect "Zen dog" I'd like to be. Plenty of things throw me off-kilter and make me feel less than a success. Things like the sudden arrival of a new two-legged little sister. I admit that I was a handful when I was a puppy, but I had no idea that such a little human could be the source of so much chaos and confusion. Whether it's sharing the previously undivided attention of my humans or being herded around the house by a tyrannical toddler, there are days when I feel anything but well adjusted.

And yet, every night I curl up on my dog bed and drift off to sleep knowing that my day was a success and that *I* was a success. Humans like to say that "every dog has her day," hinting that everyone has a chance at success at some point in their lives. But once again, humans have their dog idioms all mixed up. Success isn't a one-shot deal. Success is something that *every* dog makes happen *every* day.

You see, chasing success for its own sake is a lot like chasing your own tail—even if you manage to catch it (not an easy feat for a stub-tailed dog like me), you can't hold on to it for very long. Worse, if your eyes are always fixated on something else, you'll miss the small victories of life that are right under your nose. The only true path to success is living an honest, authentic life, where the things you do and the decisions you make are in sync with who you are and what you value. I like to think of success as a good game of tug-of-war: Sometimes you pull the rope toy closer toward you and sometimes you watch it slip away. The rope toy never stays balanced for very long, and that's

OK—as long as you play the game with focus, determination, strength, balance, teamwork and a sense of fun.

I hope this book prompts humans to slow down and tune in to the four-legged teachers (dogs!) who have so much to share about living successful, well-balanced lives. Dachshunds, beagles and greyhounds do things differently, but they do it the way it works best for them. All you can do is be the best dog (or human) that you can be. Start by asking the questions that a smart dog would ask herself:

- Do I know what makes my life "zoom"?

- Do I do what's best for my body and mind?

- Do I search for the positive side of things?

- Do I focus my attention on what matters?

- Do I listen carefully and communicate clearly?

- Do I follow my instincts and go after my goals?

- Do I build relationships with the people around me?

- Do I show appreciation for what I have?

- Do I make time to laugh and to play?

- Do I try to be present in my own life and in the lives of others?

Sure, these are deep questions. Do they all have to be answered "yes" to have a successful life? Of course not. My answers change every day, because life is messy and unpredictable. It's also spontaneous, joyful and exciting. Asking the questions puts me back on track so that every night I curl up on my pillow and sleep soundly, knowing I did the best I could do and was the best boxer I could be.

Here's to you wonderful humans being the best people you can be. My parting advice? Be real. Be authentic. If you can't be a dog, be human.

A Bella Life

Afterword by Ellen Galvin and Patrick Galvin

Bella the boxer joined our family when she was just 8 weeks old. Since then, she's rarely left our side and has helped us become better people, parents and business leaders. We are grateful for her unconditional love and for everything she's taught us about leading authentic, successful lives.

Still, it hasn't always been ideal. Of course, we thought having her with us in the office all day long would be easy. We had visions of an obedient, adoring puppy lying silently at our feet while we tended to our clients' needs. We clearly underestimated the amount of work required to run a business while training a stubborn, rambunctious boxer.

Bella tested our patience and wreaked havoc on our carpets and our work schedules. We started scheduling client calls between potty breaks and midday trips to the dog park. We learned to type with one hand while using the other to throw the slobbery tennis balls and stuffed animals that she dropped at our feet (over and over and over again). We drove to well-pet exams and obedience classes—all to ensure that our fur baby would grow into the healthy, well-mannered adult dog that she is today.

At first, the disruptions left us feeling scattered and unproductive. Before Bella, we easily filled 12 to 14-hour workdays. After Bella, we were lucky to get a few hours of solid, focused time per day. "How did a 10-pound puppy turn our world upside down?" we asked each other. Yet, miraculously, after settling into our new routines, we started getting *more* work done than before.

What had happened? The simple explanation is that with fewer hours per day for getting our "real" work done, we were forced to work more efficiently. We spent less time surfing the Internet, stopped making unnecessary calls and ignored the e-mails that weren't directly related to our work at hand.

More important, something had happened on a deeper level. Suddenly, we had a legitimate excuse to step outside the office a few times a day. Our furry, four-legged magnet introduced us to people and places we hadn't known about before. We made new friends, acquired professional contacts and established connections to the community (Bella being the unofficial mayor of a few different streets around town). We don't have anything against technology, really—without it we wouldn't be in business. But Bella became a daily reminder of how important it is to connect with people on a real level, beyond the four corners of a computer screen.

Bella also brought levity into the office and taught us that it's OK to do great work without taking our jobs or ourselves too seriously. For example, we debated for weeks whether to include Bella's biography on our corporate website. Even though we thought we were being awfully clever and fun, we worried that clients and prospects might consider it unprofessional. Thankfully, our fears were unfounded. Someone made the comment that Bella had turned our website into something "delightfully human" (isn't it interesting that it takes a dog to humanize us sometimes?). One client sent us photos of his Boston terriers, another reminisced about his beloved German shepherds and a third regaled us with the exploits of her naughty Newfoundland.

Indeed, dogs are great for keeping the ego in check because they don't care about your titles or accomplishments. In fact, dogs are the ultimate equalizers because people *everywhere* love to talk about their dogs, from the CEO in the boardroom, to the barista in the local coffee shop, to the homeless person living on the street. They know that their dogs love them no matter who they are, what they look like or what they do for a living.

All too often, we humans get stuck in the stress and routine of daily life. We become the center of our own little universe. Sometimes, it takes a Bella to shake things up and help us create a new way of living and working. If we just pay attention to them being dogs, we learn so much— curiosity, resilience, gratitude and connection. It doesn't matter whether dogs have the same emotions and feelings as humans, we can still see their lives as examples for our own. By letting them show us what it means to be a dog, instead of trying to make them human, we just might find the success and life balance we've been searching for.

We hope this book, and Bella's wisdom, will help you unleash your potential and create your own success.

Notes

Success and a New Breed of Working Dog

According to the American Pet Products Association in its 2009–2010 National Pet Owners Survey, there are more than 77 million dogs in American homes.

The statistics on dog owners who talk to their dogs on the phone come from the 2004 Pet Study by the American Animal Hospital Association.

The survey of dog-loving CEOs is discussed in "Dog-Loving CEOs Have a Few Tips for the Obamas and Bo," by Del Jones, *USA Today*, April 13, 2009.

An interview with Christopher Mattaliano of the Portland Opera appeared in "Dogs and Cats Are Welcome at Some Portland Workplaces," by Jacques Von Lunen, *The Oregonian*, May 19, 2009. Replacements Ltd.'s dog policy was detailed in "Dogs Allowed: Creature Comforts at the Workplace," by Sharon L. Peters, *USA Today*, February 24, 2009.

The statistics on the number of Americans working from home are laid out in *Microtrends: The Small Forces Behind Tomorrow's Big Changes*, by Mark Penn and E. Kinney Zalesne (New York: Twelve, 2007).

According to a 2006 survey of working Americans 18 and older conducted by the American Pet Products Association, one in five U.S. companies allows pets in the workplace. The survey also found that significant numbers believe having a pet in the workplace leads to increased creativity (55 million), decreased absenteeism (53 million), better relationships among co-workers (50 million), higher productivity (38 million) and improved employee/manager relationships (37 million). In addition, 46 million people who bring their pets to the workplace work longer hours.

Chapter 1 • Purpose: Discover What Makes You Zoom

Ellen Galvin interviewed Claire DeJesus, mom to Emmi the pug, and Julie Burk, Zadok's two-legged partner in animal therapy work, in July and August 2009.

Amy Sacks, founder and executive director of the Pixie Project (*www.pixieproject.org*), spoke with Ellen Galvin in July 2009. The Pixie Project is named for a terrier mix that Amy rescued from an Iowa puppy mill and brought home to be adopted by her parents, Ann and Robert Sacks.

Ellen Galvin and Patrick Galvin interviewed Carol Gardner, founder of Zelda Wisdom (*www.zeldawisdom.com*), in August 2009.

Chapter 2 • Body: Stretch Your Lungs, Stretch Your Limbs

Patrick Galvin interviewed Al Lee in June 2009. Lee and co-author Don Campbell wrote *Perfect Breathing: Transform Your Life One Breath at a Time* (New York: Sterling Publishing, 2009).

The National Center for Health Statistics, which is part of the Centers for Disease Control and Prevention, reports that more than 34 percent of Americans were obese in 2005–2006. The survey included 4,356 adults over age 20 who take part in a regular government survey of health.

The numbers on dog obesity come from the 2008 U.S. Pet Obesity Study conducted by the Association for Pet Obesity Prevention. Founded in 2005 by Dr. Ernie Ward, veterinarian and competitive Ironman triathlete, the group is dedicated to reducing pet obesity and is not affiliated with any veterinary industry corporation or business.

An interview with obesity expert Dr. James Levine of the Mayo Clinic appeared in "Q&A: How to Drop Pounds

With All-Day Activities, Not Exercise," by Nanci Hellmich, *USA Today*, January 22, 2009.

For advice on putting together your own walking program, read *Fitness Unleashed: A Dog and Owner's Guide to Losing Weight and Gaining Health Together*, by Marty Becker, DVM, and Robert Kushner, MD (New York: Three Rivers Press, 2006).

A study of 200 people at three major corporations revealed that an employee's quality of life, mental performance and time management was 15 percent better on days when they exercised. A 2004 study in the Journal of Occupational and Environmental Medicine shows that people who increase their physical activity also improve the quality of their work and overall job performance.

Ellen Galvin interviewed Jill Bowers, co-founder of Thank Dog! Bootcamp (*www.thankdogbootcamp.com*), in November 2009.

Results of a survey of smokers who were also pet owners were reported in the medical journal *Tobacco Control*, based on a 2009 online survey conducted by researchers at the Henry Ford Health System.

Chapter 3 • Attitude: Make Happiness Happen

A survey from the American Pet Products Association found that approximately 62 percent of pet owners keep their animals in the house at night. Of those, nearly half the cats and one-third of the dogs sleep on their humans' bed.

Sonja Lyubomirsky is a professor of psychology at the University of California, Riverside, who concluded that happiness is 50 percent genetic, 40 percent intentional and 10 percent circumstantial. Her work is explained in "C'mon, Get Happy," by Marnell Jameson, *The Los Angeles Times*, September 8, 2008.

Ellen Galvin and Patrick Galvin attended a happiness seminar conducted by Rick Foster and Greg Hicks (*www .fosterhicks.com*) in Antarctica in December 2008 (yes, Antarctica—it's a long story), and interviewed Rick Foster again in July 2009. He and Greg co-authored *How We Choose to Be Happy: The 9 Choices of Extremely Happy People— Their Secrets, Their Stories* (New York: Perigee, 2000).

Ellen Galvin interviewed Mimi Ausland, who founded *FreeKibble.com* and *FreeKibbleKat.com* when she was just 11 years old, in October 2009.

On the topic of humor, Ellen Galvin interviewed Ben Huh and Gail Hand in October 2009. Ben Huh is the CEO of Pet Holdings, the media empire that runs the *I Can Has Cheezburger* website, among several others. Gail Hand is a stand-up comedian turned motivational humorist whose four dogs are part of her curriculum (*www.gailhand.com*).

Chapter 4 • Focus: Keep Your Eyes on the Ball
According to the Centers for Disease Control and Prevention, nearly 30 percent of Americans are habitually getting less than six hours of sleep a night—far less than the recommended seven to nine hours—and an estimated 50–70 million people suffer from sleep disorders or constant sleep loss. According to the 2009 Sleep in America poll, conducted annually by the National Sleep Foundation, 64 percent of adults in the United States have trouble sleeping a few nights a week, and 41 percent say it is a nightly occurrence. Nearly one-fourth of the patients at the Mayo Clinic Sleep Disorders Center who have insomnia admit to sharing their bed with a four-legged housemate.

Ellen interviewed Marci Alboher (*www.heymarci.com*) in May 2009. Alboher is the author of *One Person/Mul-*

tiple Careers: A New Model for Work/Life Success (New York: Warner Books, 2007).

The list of items surgically removed from pets comes from Veterinary Pet Insurance, the nation's oldest and largest provider of pet health insurance (and Bella's insurer).

Chapter 5 • Communication: Sit, Stay and Listen

When asked, "Who listens to you best?" the majority of pet owners surveyed by the American Animal Hospital Association chose their pet. Only 30 percent chose their spouse or significant other, and another 25 percent chose a friend or family member.

Amy Sutherland's book is *What Shamu Taught Me About Life, Love, and Marriage* (New York: Random House, 2008).

A study on the correlation between good posture and self-confidence appears in the October 2009 issue of the *European Journal of Social Psychology*.

Information on nonverbal communication was provided by Doug Duncan, certified dog trainer and owner of Doggy Business Dog Training & Lodging (*www.doggybusiness.net*), in April 2010.

Chapter 6 • Persistence: Never Let Go of the Rope

Bella interviewed Courage the cat in August 2009 with assistance from his humans, Andrea Waltz and Richard Fenton, authors of *Go for No!* (4th ed., Courage Crafters, 2007).

In his bestselling book *Outliers: The Story of Success* (New York: Little, Brown and Company, 2008), Malcolm Gladwell refers to the "10,000-Hour Rule" which states that the key to success in any field is a matter of practicing a specific task for around 10,000 hours.

In October 2009, Ellen interviewed Joe Roetheli, who created Greenies dog treats with his wife, Judy. Additional information came from "The Dog Who Breathed a New Business," by Brent Bowers, *The New York Times*, June 6, 2007; and "Roetheli's Evergreen Persistence Drives Life," by Rob Roberts, *Kansas City Business Journal*, April 27, 2007.

Chapter 7 • Camaraderie: Build Your Pack

The role of volunteerism in extending lifespan is addressed in a study of 6,360 older people by scientists at the University of California at San Francisco. The study found that those who volunteer were half as likely to die during the four-year study as those who did not.

James V. O'Connor's "Puppies Behind Bars" appeared in *The New York Times*, August 22, 1999.

An account of Tarra and Bella's friendship can be found on the Elephant Sanctuary's website at *www.elephants.com* as well as in "Big Love: In Tennessee, Dogs Are an Elephant's Best Friends" by Megan McMurray, *The Bark*, November/December 2008.

Ellen Galvin interviewed Cathy King, DVM PhD, CEO and founder of World Vets (*www.worldvets.org*), in April 2010.

Chapter 8 • Appreciation: Shake It Like You Mean It

Corinne Dowling, founder of the canine enrichment program Give a Dog a Bone (*www.gadab.org*), spoke with Ellen Galvin in June and July 2009.

The entire story of the Rev. Will Bowen is detailed at *www.acomplaintfreeworld.org*. Additional information was provided by A Complaint Free World's Autumn Page, March 2010.

The ratio of self-storage facilities to the number of Starbucks in this country is 7:1, and one out of 10 U.S. households rents a storage unit (statistics taken from "The Self-Storage Self," by Jon Mooallem, *The New York Times*, September 2, 2009).

For 2010, the American Pet Products Association predicts total U.S. pet industry expenditures of $47.7 billion, double the amount spent just a decade ago.

The link between thankfulness and good health is from research done by the University of California, Davis; it shows that people who compiled a weekly gratitude journal exercised for 80 minutes more per week than people who did not.

"Rescuing Gracie," the story of Jim and Sherry Packard and their dog, Gracie, appeared in *Success From Home*, October 2008 (Vol. 4, Issue 10). Sherry Packard provided additional information and anecdotes in October 2009.

Chapter 9 • Play: Stop and Eat the Roses

Watching TV accounted for half of all Americans' leisure time in 2008, according to the Bureau of Labor Statistics. The Nielsen Co.'s "Three Screen Report" (which refers to televisions, computers and cell phones) for the fourth quarter of 2008 said the average American watches more than 151 hours of TV a month. That's approximately five hours a day, and a record high.

The science of play is examined thoroughly in "Taking Play Seriously," by Robin Marantz Henig, *The New York Times*, February 17, 2008. An interview with play expert Dr. Stuart Brown was recorded on July 24, 2008, for American Public Media's *Speaking of Faith with Krista Tippett*. More information is available from the National Institute of Play (*www.nifplay.org*).

Kyoko Nakayama and Anthony Sandberg were interviewed in June 2009 and September 2009.

Chapter 10 • Presence: Cheese the Moment

Ellen Galvin interviewed Dr. Laird Goodman, DVM,

board member of the Delta Society (*www.deltasociety.org*), in November 2009.

Ellen Galvin interviewed Larry Chusid of The Pongo Fund (*www.thepongofund.org*) in November 2009. Additional details are found in "For the Love of Pongo, Portland Donor Provides Meals for Pets," by Tom Hallman, *The Oregonian*, July 29, 2009; and "Pet Food Bank Decades in the Making," by Jacques Von Lunen, *The Oregonian*, November 3, 2009.

Contributors

A tremendous thank you to everyone who contributed their time, energy and words of wisdom, including the following people and fabulous dogs who are referenced in the order in which they appear. Please check out their websites where listed to see how you can support their amazing work.

Claire DeJesus and her rescue pug, Emmi, who work together as a therapy team to bring comfort to hospice patients in Nevada.

Zadok, the 81-pound Akita who travels across the country with his two-legged human, Julie Burk, as part of a crisis intervention therapy team.

Amy Sacks, founder of the Pixie Project, a nonprofit animal adoption center and retail pet supply store in Portland, Ore.: *www.pixieproject.org.*

Carol Gardner, the creative genius behind the Zelda Wisdom brand: *www.zeldawisdom.com.*

Al Lee, professional speaker, author and expert on the subject of proper breathing: *www.perfectbreathing.com.*

Jill Bowers, co-founder of Thank Dog! Bootcamp: *www.thankdogbootcamp.com.*

Jenny Walker, in Portland, Ore., who motivates her students to exercise with her positive energy while kicking their butts at the same time.

Rick Foster and Greg Hicks, best-selling authors and consultants in the fields of health, happiness and team dynamics: *www.fosterhicks.com.*

Mimi Ausland, founder of *www.freekibble.com* and *www.freekibblekat.com* and hero to hungry, homeless animals across the country.

Motivational humorist Gail Hand and her canine clan, Desi, Lucy, Zippy and Zoe: *www.gailhand.com.*

Ben Huh, CEO of the Seattle-based Cheezburger Network: *www.cheezburger.com.*

Marci Alboher, author, speaker and companion to Sinatra, Manhattan's savviest French bulldog: *www.heymarci.com.*

Doug Duncan, certified dog trainer and owner (with his wife, Meredith Wilson) of Doggy Business Dog Training & Lodging in Portland, Ore.: *www.doggybusiness.net.*

Courage the cat, whose humans, Richard Fenton and Andrea Waltz, are the creators/authors of Go for No!: *www.goforno.com.*

Joe and Judy Roetheli, philanthropists and the inventors of Greenies products for pets: *www.lilredfoundation.com.*

Cathy King, DVM PhD, and CEO and founder of World Vets: *www.worldvets.org.*

Corinne Dowling, founder of Give a Dog a Bone, a quality-of-life program for San Francisco's shelter dogs: *www.gadab.org.*

Rev. Will Bowen and his staff at A Complaint Free World: *www.acomplaintfreeworld.org.*

Jim Packard and Sherry Packard, for sharing their stories about Gracie the cocker spaniel and the lessons she taught them about the power of appreciation: *www.jimpackard.com.*

Kyoko Nakayama, dog trainer, photographer and manager of Tor Johnson Photography in Hawaii: *www.tjhawaii.com.*

Anthony Sandberg, founder and president of OCSC SAILING in Berkeley, Calif.: *www.ocsc.com.*
Laird Goodman, DVM, and a member of the board of directors at the Delta Society: *www.deltasociety.org.*
Larry Chusid, founder of The Pongo Fund and The Pongo Fund Pet Food Bank, helping keep pets and their families together in Portland, Ore.: *www.thepongofund.org.*

Acknowledgments

I could not have written this book without the support of a large group of family and friends of both the furry and nonfurry persuasion.

First, I'd like to thank my two-legged humans for helping me get my words onto paper and for their ongoing support in the form of long walks, yummy treats and belly rubs. I'm grateful to Adam Bacher of Adam Bacher Photography (*www.adambacher.com*), who took time out between important photojournalism trips to Rwanda to shoot many of the photos that accompany this book and who bribed me with lots of cheese in order to capture the shots. Credit also goes to Robyn M Fritz at Alchemy West (*www.alchemywestinc.com*), whose editorial prowess and intuitive understanding of humans and dogs helped whip my ideas into shape. I'd also like to thank Robert Lanphear of Lanphear Design (*www.lanpheardesign.com*) for designing the book's cover and interior, and Laurel Robinson of Laurel Robinson Editorial Services (*www.laurel copyeditor.com*) for her copyediting services.

I'm thankful to Terri Pope and Randy Pope, of Mi-T's Boxers in Dallas, Ore., for giving me all the advantages of a good head start and for being ethical and responsible promoters of the breed. I especially love being invited to stay with them and their big, boisterous brood of boxers whenever my humans indulge their need to travel to wacky, faraway places like Antarctica. I wonder whether they would be willing to board Mom and Dad when I go out of town on a book-signing tour.

I'd also like to acknowledge all the smart, kind and hardworking business owners who have become part of my routine and given me ideas and examples aplenty for this book. These include Keri Burnidge and her staff at Dogs In the City, Doug Duncan and Meredith Wilson of Doggy Business Dog Training & Lodging, Kim Hormby and James Taylor at Stay Pet Hotel, and Mike Mallar and Christine Mallar of Green Dog Pet Supply. It also includes the very nice people at Laurelhurst Veterinary Hospital in Portland, Ore., who give me cookies whenever they draw my blood or otherwise poke and prod me in the name of good health. Indeed, their veterinary services were invaluable in what my humans now refer to as "the regrettable ham incident." Let's just say that boxers and ham are not a good combination, no matter how much we plead and beg for just one more morsel.

Last but not least, I am lucky to live in one of the most dog-friendly places on the planet. In a city with more dogs than children, the people of Portland, Ore., are obsessed with their four-legged fur babies. It's not all about play-dates and designer dog gear, although there are plenty of options available for the pooch who likes to be pampered. Portland's dogs and humans are fortunate to have organizations like the Oregon Humane Society (OHS), a state-of-the-art facility with an adoption rate that is more than double the national average. (In 2009, OHS set a new annual record for number of adoptions (10,017) and percentage of lives saved (96 percent). Appropriately, the 10,000th animal to be adopted was a dog named Bella.)

This rate is particularly impressive when you consider that it includes animals transferred from 48 other animal welfare agencies throughout Oregon, Washington and California—animals who are given a second chance at finding a home when time and resources run out elsewhere. Moreover, the efforts of OHS and its supporters have helped Oregon create some of the nation's toughest animal cruelty laws, including federal penalties for abuse, theft and dog fighting. The Animal Legal Defense Fund ranks Oregon among the top five in the nation for protecting the rights of animals.

I hope that someday dogs and humans everywhere will have affordable and convenient access to such stellar resources. Unfortunately, we still have a long way to go—which is why I am donating 10 percent of the profits from this book to the various animal welfare organizations mentioned here, so they may continue the award-winning programs that make them role models for other nonprofit organizations around the globe.

Last, I want to thank all of the dog lovers and savvy businesspeople who didn't blink an eye when asked to be interviewed by a dog. My humans and I learned a great deal from each of your stories and suggestions, and we'll be sharing them and more on our blog at our website: *www.secretsofaworkingdog.com*. If you have a story to share or just want to reach out and say "woof," drop me a line at *bella@secretsofaworkingdog.com*.

Bella the Boxer

Index

About the Authors

Bella the Boxer

Bella belongs to the breed category known as a working dog. But this dog doesn't herd sheep. Instead, she's the director of goodwill (D.O.G.) at Galvin Communications, a word of mouth marketing firm in Portland, Ore., that helps organizations break through the clutter and spark conversations that get tails and tongues wagging. In the office, Bella maintains a sense of energy, enthusiasm and creativity while making sure that her two-legged co-workers don't spend all day hiding behind their computer screens.

Typical of her breed, Bella is a fun-loving spirit who is happiest when like-minded dogs and their people surround her. She believes that too many humans are overworked and overstressed in this fast-paced 24/7 world. After dispensing advice to her own humans for years, Bella decided it was time to help busy people everywhere learn how thinking like a dog is the quickest and easiest path to a successful, well-balanced life.

(Note: Bella would like to point out that any examples of bad working habits found in this book are purely coincidental and have absolutely, positively nothing to do with her co-authors. After all, the first secret to success is never to bite the hand that feeds you.)

To follow Bella's ongoing adventures and get more ideas and examples on how to create success in work and life by thinking like a dog, visit *www.secretsofaworkingdog.com*.

Ellen Galvin

Ellen is an accomplished writer with a talent for sniffing out a good news story. As the chief wordsmith of Galvin Communications, she has placed clients in media outlets ranging from *The Wall Street Journal* to *Outside* magazine to *WineSpectator.com*. She co-authored a popular pet blog that was featured online at *The New York Times*, and her travel articles have appeared in airline magazines, regional newspapers and adventure travel sites.

Although she loves all animals, Ellen has a soft spot for the boisterous boxer who has a knack for humorously getting to the heart of what matters in life. She has an MBA from the Walter A. Haas School of Business at the University of California, Berkeley. In addition to translating for her dog Bella, she speaks French, German and a smattering of Spanish.

Patrick Galvin

As the chief galvanizer of Galvin Communications, Patrick helps organizations communicate with customers, prospects, journalists, and bloggers in creative ways that strengthen relationships. He also speaks to companies and associations on how they can draw upon Bella's ideas to achieve greater levels of success.

Patrick has presented to hundreds of groups throughout the United States, Canada, and Latin America and is the past president of the Oregon Chapter of the National Speakers Association. He graduated with an MBA in international marketing from Thunderbird and is fluent in Spanish and Portuguese. As Bella is Patrick's first pet larger than a goldfish, he is just learning how to speak dog.